MW00714395

Contents

CULTIVATING SUCCESS   49

Introduction

Building Success

Becky Jo Peterson

As I stood on the stage holding hands with my fellow Junior Miss participants, I found it hard to believe that only a few years earlier I'd held the hands of my mother and sisters as we fled in the middle of the night to a safe haven. Then, we were escaping physical and emotional abuse of an alcoholic stepfather. Now, I was on the path to discovering what the future held for me. For years I lived with the fear and insecurity that my past forced upon me. But now, learning that five judges chose me to represent a group of outstanding young women from my hometown at California's state program, I began to wonder what they saw in me that was so special. Their decision forced me to believe that I must have something to offer the world. It was my obligation to discover it, to take advantage of the opportunities for personal enrichment and scholarships, and to believe in myself. Distinguished Young Women, formerly America's Junior Miss, provided me with opportunity, provided the funds for continued education, and solidified the path to a successful, fulfilling life.

Success is a relative term. It is defined by the World English Dictionary as "the favorable outcome of something attempted or the attainment of wealth and fame." Google the word "success," and within .25 seconds you get almost three million hits with advice on how to achieve it, how to define it, and how to become like those who have reached it. Yet, when you bring it to the personal level, each of us would most likely define and measure the word success in a unique way.

Each of the contributing authors in this book is a former participant in what is now called Distinguished Young Women—just a few of the more than 700,000 intelligent and accomplished women who have participated since 1958. Though many of these women did win scholarship money, they state that what they gained most from the program was confidence, ambition, and friendships. Their essays vary by topic, and they each provide a unique perspective on how to cultivate success; yet, these successful women agree that success is in large part deterred by becoming their best personal selves.

Distinguished Young Women itself exemplifies success. The program that was founded more than half a century ago by the Mobile Junior Chamber of Commerce had a meager beginning with just 18 contestants and a small amount of scholarship money. Today, the program provides more than $63 million in cash and college scholarship opportunities *each year* to thousands of young women across the nation who take part in the program. More than 17,000 individuals volunteer their time and resources to produce more than 450 local programs, 50 state programs, and the National Finals each year.

Throughout history, Distinguished Young Women has remained true to its purpose: to empower, recognize, and reward young women for their accomplishments. The path has not always been easy, as the program has been criticized for remaining true to its wholesome values. Nevertheless, the caliber of women who are impacted by our program demonstrates the effect that Distinguished Young Women has on the lives of its participants and volunteers.

One of the hallmarks of success is the ability to continue performing well through decades of change. To do that, change itself must be embraced with open arms. Distinguished Young Women has continued to adapt to the new millennium by changing its name from America's Junior Miss to Distinguished Young Women, by emphasizing the program's focus on scholarship, and by making minor production changes that better showcase the accomplishments of the program's participants. The Board of Directors is confident that these changes will help to ensure that Distinguished Young Women continues to impact young women in the future as it has for more than fifty years.

The achievements of the 27 amazing women who have contributed to this book are just glimpses of the success that our participants have achieved. We invite you to read more as others are sharing their stories at *www.DistinguishedYW.org*. Distinguished Young Women truly changes the lives of young women, providing them with opportunities for scholarships, personal development, and networking as they work to reach their goals.

Becky Jo Peterson is the Executive Director for Distinguished Young Women (formerly America's Junior Miss), a national scholarship program for high school girls. She was Napa Valley's Junior Miss in 1975 and one of ten finalists at California's Junior Miss. Becky Jo came from a textbook example of an abusive childhood, and her Junior Miss experience encouraged her to find her own success. Her experience as a participant, volunteer, and California's state chairman, as well as her degree in Business Management, made her uniquely qualified to become Executive Director in December of 2005 after the program was on the brink of closure. She is passionate about two causes: helping young women to achieve their educational and life goals, and preventing child and spousal abuse. While in Napa, she worked as the Industry and Member Relations Director for the Napa Valley Vintners trade association for wineries. She enjoyed her role in helping to preserve the rural and agricultural culture of the Napa Valley, creating housing for migrant farmworkers, and determining the local charities to receive grants in excess of $6 million annually raised by the Napa Valley Wine Auction.

Becky Jo continues to find leadership opportunities as a member of the Mobile Chamber of Commerce and as a board member of the Girl Scouts of South Alabama. She is also a guest speaker on the topics of volunteerism and domestic abuse.

Becky Jo is married to the nicest man on earth, glass artist Ed Edwards. They have a married daughter, who lives in Southern California. Becky Jo and Ed both enjoy wine and food pairing, cooking, and traveling— especially to Italy!

What Is Success?

1

"I Haven't Done That, Yet."

Madison Leonard

As I lined up at the front of the stage with nine other state representatives on the final program night in Mobile, Alabama, I was incredulous of the results that would be read only minutes later. My body ached from the fitness routine that we had performed an hour earlier, my heart pounded so hard I was sure it was audible to the audience, and standing up straight in those high-heeled shoes became an increasingly difficult task. Suddenly, two finalists were announced—two of my close friends! As my mind wrapped around my joy for them, a buzzing silence filled the room. The announcement of the winner was about to come. The emcee declared, "From Idaho, Madison Leonard!" and from that moment on, my life has been changed.

Being named the first Distinguished Young Woman of America was astonishing—a complete honor, of course—but astonishing. I would never have predicted such an outcome after traveling to Nationals in Mobile and competing for two weeks with some of the highest achieving young women in the country. How could I have forecasted such a thing? The 49 girls I was privileged enough to meet were absolutely incredible: off-the-charts brilliant, talented in a multitude of ways, aware of and engaged in the world, personable, and humble. So one can see how being chosen as the representative of these amazing young women, their states, and the scores of local programs in all those states is astonishing. Naturally, I could never break down how the judges decided that I would be an adequate representative of such an inspiring group, but I do know how the effort that I've put forth into my multifaceted goals and passions led me to my version of success. Pop culture says that success is a simple combination of any of the following elements: monetary wealth, prestige, and power. However, truly successful individuals breach all lines of shallow affluence and unsatisfying fame, proving that the recipe for success involves much more than trivial matters of money and status. With only eighteen years of life under my belt, (and only the last four months of those years spent on my own!), I am certainly no expert on matters of success. There is no long line of persons, as far as I know, anxiously awaiting words of wisdom from a first-year college student. But through some personal experiments, I've discovered methods to achieve success in my own life.

"Jack of All Trades"

Growing up, my loving parents were crazy enough to allow me to try just about every sport and activity that was available to me as a kid. The mantra in our family was never "I can't do that," but rather, "I haven't done that YET." This calculated into hours of basketball practice, piano lessons, dance classes, theater rehearsals, and a myriad of other activities every week. The main goals of this cornucopia of frenetic activity were fun and experience. I suppose my parents began to realize after a mere eight points scored over four years of basketball that I was not particularly gifted athletically and would probably not need a sports agent in the future. And despite my whining over repeating boring scales on the piano, they continued to encourage me to learn the instrument. These habits of discipline and commitment followed me into high school, where I continued stuffing my weekly schedule with theater rehearsals, tennis matches, student leadership, voice lessons, volunteer work, and various other clubs. Of course, homework was still the priority in our home, but I genuinely enjoyed being busy and learning more every day.

However, before I continue, I should clarify that in no way was I the absolute best at all of these activities. I was cut from the freshman volleyball team, lost two student government elections, and went 3–4 in my last tennis season. Over my high school career, I insisted on trying a wide variety of activities knowing that some of these small failures would arise. I found out early that while I might not be the best at something, I could be comfortably proficient in almost everything, or certainly most things. Although receiving a smaller role in the play my senior year stung at first, I learned how to keep a positive attitude and improve my acting on stage. Even when I lost tennis matches, I discovered how to be a first-class team player and made habits to maintain an active lifestyle.

By testing myself in areas of my life that might be considered weaknesses and soaking up all types of activities, I made myself a "jack of all trades" and now have life experience in many different areas. More likely than not, I will never be a professional basketball player, but I am a more well-rounded and seasoned individual just for testing my personal limits in an arena in which I doubted I would ever be a superstar. We live in a time when scholarships, college acceptance, employment, and many other opportunities are granted to individuals with a variety of abilities and experience. Future success will depend on what you've done, what you're doing now, and what you are willing to learn to do.

Speak and Listen

One of my favorite historical figures, Winston Churchill, once said, "Courage is what it takes to stand up and speak; courage is also what it takes to sit down and listen." Over the past few years, this quote has reminded me to maintain two distinct habits in my daily life: to communicate my opinion and to be receptive of the knowledge that that crosses my path every day. While I cannot know the exact intention of Churchill's statement, I can assume that if a man who worked as a diplomat for a living found it necessary to both speak and listen, it must be important.

Communication skills are absolutely necessary for success. From the very beginning of our lives, we communicate through sounds and speech; and as we grow, we accumulate more knowledge to form our own opinions. At some point, outside influences try to stifle our opinions. As a result, many teenagers succumb to this pressure and become indifferent and incommunicative. But in order to be heard and make a stand for important beliefs in your own life, you have to communicate! Speak up about your school's policies, maintain good interaction with your teachers or coworkers, or maybe write a letter to your local newspaper about something you find important. We have so many wonderful privileges in this country, and we should exercise our right of free speech daily.

Being an extrovert, I have never had much difficulty voicing my thoughts and opinions. For this reason, the second half of Churchill's statement has always been a learning tool and gentle reminder in my life. Just as it is critical to open your mouth and voice your thoughts, it's equally essential to close it and give others the opportunity to speak. Listening to contrasting opinions and alternative perspectives gives an incredible amount of insight to any topic and deepens the level of knowledge that we can have on a subject. Personally, the most insightful concepts that I have ever absorbed have come from others, not from me. The ability to listen and appreciate the two parts of a balanced conversation will come in handy in our family relationships, education, friendships, employment, marriage, community interactions, parenthood, government, and so on. Many of us have heard the old adage about the genius of being designed with TWO ears and only ONE mouth. Very early in life, I found out that by listening closely, people would often times tell me what they had learned, what mistakes they had made, what made them laugh or cry, and what influenced them for good or bad. Being a successful individual is the result of being a successful member of the whole of society. Having the courage to both speak and listen will aid in that endeavor.

In many ways, I have experienced more failures and mistakes than successes. But in a way, those disappointments and mishaps have been the fertile soil from which has sprouted the vast majority of my achievements to date. Without trying basketball, I would never have known if sports were possible for me and may never have tried the performing arts. Without losing student elections, I may never have realized the way my self-confidence can carry me through discouraging moments. Without speaking up, I may never have known that my voice has the potential to inspire others. Without listening, I may have missed the key elements I needed to lead me down the road to success. Although I only have a few months of adulthood under my belt, I look forward to determining my own successes in the future. And I am convinced that this will take place as I continue to try new things, to communicate well, and to listen to the advice and opinions of others.

Madison Leonard of Idaho is the 53rd young woman to win the program's overall award, but she is the first Distinguished Young Woman. In addition to Madison's down-to-earth personality and ability to articulate her thoughts, her vocal rendition of the jazzy number, "The Nearness of You," while accompanying herself on the piano, impressed both the audience and the judges.

Madison graduated from Coeur d'Alene High School, where she was salutatorian, participated in musical theater, and was a member of the varsity tennis team. Through the local, state, and national programs, Madison won more than $50,000 in scholarship funds.

Madison is the program's first-ever national winner from Idaho. She attends Pepperdine University and studies music performance and journalism.

2

The Road to Success

Jean Bokelmann, M.D.

It seems to me that the meaning of success has changed since I was a senior in high school. If you look at page 159 of my high school yearbook, you will find a picture of me under the heading, "Most Likely to Succeed." As I recall, in 1971 the common definition of success was having a powerful job, eventually landing "the corner office," having a lifetime of secure earnings, and maintaining the respect and admiration of one's peers. If one accepts that definition of success, my high school classmates who voted me to receive this title were not in error in their prediction. By all outward appearances, my life has been a successful one. I won the scholastic achievement award at the 1971 America's Junior Miss scholarship program. With the scholarship money, I was able to afford the tuition at Stanford University, where I graduated early in 1975. I went directly to medical school at Case Western Reserve University, where I graduated in 1980. After serving a commission in the Indian Health Service, I went on to achieve board certification in Family Medicine and, subsequently, a certificate of added qualifications in Geriatrics. For the past 15 years, I have been an associate professor of Family Medicine and the director of a student health center. I have played an important role in the lives of my patients. I have enjoyed a rewarding family life and have raised two sons who are now independent young adults. I have kept myself relatively healthy through good food and regular exercise. I have nurtured my spiritual growth through introspection, exploration, study, and meditation. My retirement nest egg continues to look promising. I believe I fit the 1971definition of "success." Yet, I don't feel at all ready to pat myself on the back for a job well done. I choose instead to dwell on my challenges in life, continually trying to improve upon that "most likely to succeed" woman of 1971. So, then, what truly is the meaning of this elusive concept we call "success," and why don't I feel like I'm there, yet?

Success Is a Journey

The word "succeed" originally meant "come after, go near to (*suc-* up, near + *cedere-* go)."[1] Inherent in the definition of the word is the connotation of a process rather than a state. In other words, success is always in evolution, always unfolding behind us. It is not something fixed or solid out there—a destination to be reached in its own finality. Success is however we each define it in any given moment. It is a goal—a place that we *go* toward; and the more *near* we get to this place, the more we appear to be successful. People who set more goals for themselves might be seen as more successful because they reach more goals.

Take the Risk

Thus, to be successful, one has to be willing to take calculated risks, as there are very few goals in life that come with a guarantee for success. One has to be willing to risk failure from time to time. I have failed in life on innumerable occasions. Some of my failures have been rather large in scope. I failed in my first marriage to reach my goal of staying in a committed relationship for a lifetime. Having gone through a divorce, I learned important things about myself and mustered up the courage to try again. I am now in my second marriage. To succeed in marriage, I had to allow myself to take another chance on love, to risk failing for a second time. My husband and I just celebrated our

16th wedding anniversary, and we feel closer and happier than ever. I do believe that this time in marriage I am "succeeding."

Any successful path we choose in life has hurdles to trip over. If we happen to trip and fall, we have the choice to just lie there or to hop up and get back in the race. I have not always felt successful in my profession. I have made medical mistakes that may have cost patients their health or quality of life. These mistakes have been painful lessons. Doctors are supposed to be perfect. But doctors are humans, subject to errors in judgment like the rest of the human race. In my profession, some days feel full of success, yet other days are fraught with a sense of failure. It isn't unusual for me to learn that a medication that I've prescribed for a patient only made that patient feel worse, or to realize that I've overlooked an important clue to the right diagnosis and wasted my patient's time and money going down the wrong path. At times I've wanted to quit practicing medicine because of my humanness. The stakes are so high, there is so much to know and to continue to learn, and there are unrealistic expectations that I will always do the right thing for my patients. For me, the challenge is having the courage to put that stethoscope around my neck every morning and try to be the best physician that I can be. I have to remind myself that there is a big difference between perfection (a target with an infinitely small bullseye) and success. If I can come *near* to that target, even if I'm not dead center, I have succeeded as a physician. If I give up, if I quit practicing medicine, I will be safe from the terror of making medical mistakes, but I will no longer have the opportunity every day to succeed in making my patients' lives a little better. So whenever I trip over one of those hurdles, I convince myself to get back on my feet and keep running.

There may well be lasting repercussions when one avoids taking important risks in order to avoid failure. Throughout my adulthood I've had a recurring dream that comes to me when I'm feeling particularly stressed out. In the dream, I'm facing a final exam in a world history course that I've forgotten I was taking. The textbook is immense, and I feel overwhelmed that I have to read that entire textbook in one night in order to be prepared for the exam. While there could be many interpretations of this dream, I believe the root of it goes back to ninth grade. At that time, my school offered a challenging world history course that was taught by a very stimulating and demanding teacher. He was known for not giving many A's. He wanted me to take his class. Being driven to get straight A's and believing that straight A's equaled success, I opted to take the course from an easier teacher to ensure I would get that almighty A. At some deep level, I let myself down with that decision by not rising to the challenge to learn world history at the depth my mind craved. In my decision to avoid failure, I lost out on an opportunity for growth, and I will never forget that loss.

Define Success for Yourself

Another important concept I've learned about success over the years is that other individuals and society at large can't define success for you. You have to decide for yourself what will make you feel successful with any given challenge. Motherhood is a good example. I'll be the first to admit that I haven't always been a perfect mother. There were days when I would scream or cry in exasperation. I even threw a plate at a wall once (no doubt hormones were playing a role). But overall I followed the recommendations of parenting experts to be consistent as a parent, to take responsibility for my maternal shortcomings when they arose, and to always validate my sons for the unique individuals they are. One of my sons is currently working on his doctorate, and the other has dropped out of college and is traveling the world. Some people's definition of successful motherhood may be having all of your children graduate from college and get jobs that pay a lot of money. In their eyes, I am not a successful mother. Yet, I do feel successful as a mother with regard to *both* sons because the goal I set for myself was to raise individuals who knew themselves, honored themselves, and followed their passions in life. Success is really how we define it for ourselves.

Everyone's road to success looks a little different. But common to all is the precondition that to travel on the road to success, one must be willing to risk getting a flat tire from time to time. One must be willing to make a wrong turn, back up from a dead end, and redirect. One must be willing to look human imperfection squarely in the face and ask, "Why not try?" And ultimately one must be willing to listen to one's own heart, because, in the end, only we can define our own success.

Embrace the Opportunities

Thirty-one years after being deemed "most likely to succeed," I have a different definition of success: *The ability to seize the potential for fulfillment and delight in every meaningful opportunity that presents itself in life.* Accordingly, my advice to you, as you go forth into this bold and exciting adventure that we call life, is to embrace the opportunities that call out to you. With each new challenge, ask yourself what you want from the experience. How do you define success in the task you're facing? Are the risks worth the growth and wisdom you stand to gain? Seek out your true purpose and meaning in life, then "go near to it" with all your heart. You will find that the ceaseless enticement of success will lead you to new wonders, amazing discoveries, and a richly fulfilling life.

Jean was born in Madison, Wisconsin and grew up in Las Vegas, Nevada, where she became Nevada's Junior Miss in 1971. She graduated from Stanford University with a bachelor's degree in psychology; then she went on to study at Case Western Reserve University School of Medicine, where she earned a medical degree in 1980. She completed her internship in Newport News, Virginia, followed by two years of service in the Indian Health Service on the Papago Indian Reservation in Sells, Arizona. She completed her residency in Family Medicine at UC Davis Medical Center in 1985, followed by one year of private practice in northern California. She served two additional years in the Indian Health Service, caring for Zuni and Navajo Indians in New Mexico, then moved to Pocatello, Idaho in 1988. Since 1990, she has worked for Idaho State University, where she has directed the Student Health Center and taught Family Medicine residents. Her medical areas of focus are geriatrics, women's medicine, and

integrative medicine (especially medical herbalism). Jean has raised two
sons, Sonny and Tanner, who are now off exploring and giving to the world
in their unique ways. She and her husband, Mark, enjoy numerous outdoor
activities, such as skiing and canoeing, and are developing a green energy
company together.

[1] Barnhart, R. K. (1995). *The Barnhart Concise Dictionary of Etymology.*
New York: HarperColllins.

3

Moving

Carrie Colvin Alling

As a twenty-six-year-old woman with a smidge of real-world experience under my belt, I'm noticing a transition in the way I define the word "success." I was an ambitious teen, a busy and motivated college student, and an expectant graduate. According to the traditional measures of success, I did pretty well. I made good grades, won dance competitions, and took on leadership roles. I became an expert at identifying what was expected of a "successful" person and doing just enough to win that definition for myself. It was simpler then. In high school and even in college, there are benchmarks for success that are common to all—there is a grading scale, there are first-place trophies, there are school elections to win. I may have strived toward those established marks of success, but I certainly deserve no credit for goal-setting creativity.

Then, I entered the workforce with my sights set on continued success, only to find that the mile markers on my road to success had been erased. I quickly realized that success is not some dispassionate term reserved for those who walk an established path steadily to the end. Post-school, success becomes subjective, something *defined* by the individual and *attained* by the individual.

To me, success means moving—heading off in a direction, even if the destination is unclear, but nevertheless moving with purpose, security, and hope. It is that feeling I get at the end of a long day fraught with seemingly random tasks when I hit the pillow exhausted from *moving*. I feel successful when I have used all the energy my body and mind have to offer in a day to accomplish any number of things that I believe need to be done. In my personal life, it means making sure my husband knows how much I love him by giving him time and attention. It means protecting and nurturing friendships. It even means being a good steward of the material blessings in my life by keeping our home clean and paying bills on time. In my professional life, it means doing my job effectively so that I can make life easier for others. It means leaving my to-do list shorter in the evening than it was that morning, so that when the next morning comes I feel capable instead of overwhelmed. When, God willing, I become a mother, I imagine the meaning of success will shift again. In my humble opinion, being a successful woman is simply evaluating the particular path on which you find yourself and *walking it*. You may not be able to immediately recognize the reward for your forward progress. You most likely will not receive an "A" or a trophy. In fact, rarely will your efforts to purposefully and hopefully *walk your path* even be acknowledged.

But that's not why we strive for success, anyway. Our goal should not be accolades and affirmation, trophies or positions of power. Our goal, our highest aim, should be to live the lives we've been given with purpose, security, and hope. When we do, we can be sure that, despite the disappearance of traditional mile markers, we are destined for personal, meaningful success!

Carrie Colvin Alling became America's Junior Miss in 2001 after having participated in the Jefferson County and Alabama Junior Miss programs. With the aid of her Junior Miss and National Merit scholarships, she attended Vanderbilt University in Nashville, Tennessee from 2001 to 2005. There she served as chairperson for the university's arts programming board, president of her sorority, and officer of her senior class while maintaining membership in several academic honor societies and Momentum Student Dance Group. In her senior year, she was selected to serve on the Vanderbilt University Board of Trust by her peers and a faculty committee. In May of 2005, she graduated magna cum laude *with a degree in Economics.*

Carrie moved to Los Angeles in August of that year and began working in production on the legendary television show Entertainment Tonight. *After four years and many adventures with* ET, *Carrie transitioned to a position managing nonprofit relations for TakePart, the digital media and cause marketing arm of Academy Award-winning production company, Participant Media. She resides in Los Angeles with her husband, Matt.*

4

How Far You've Come

Leslie Ann Hayashi

Dressed in gala evening wear, the audience sparkled with silver glitter, sequins, and a fabulous red dress someone dieted months to slip into. "Welcome to our thirtieth year reunion," the mistress of ceremonies announced. We sat in a fancy hotel draped in soft lighting and filled with velvet chairs. Definitely no shorts or rubber slippers. We had come a long way from the halls of our high school.

"It's great to see everyone here," the emcee continued. "We have a short program, and after that we hope everyone will reconnect with old friends and make new ones. However, before we begin, I would like to recognize one of our classmates who has made it. We knew it would happen when we voted her the 'most likely to succeed' in our senior year. And that is Judge Leslie Ann Hayashi."

While I politely listened to the applause and smiled, I did not feel I had succeeded. From my perspective, I had struggled to get through college and law school, worried about passing the bar exam, pounded the pavement to find a job, paid off student loans, and juggled married life with raising kids. Through all this, I had not thought about success—I had only thought about survival.

The truth is, before our senior year, nobody thought I was likely to succeed. Most people did not notice me and those who did considered me weird, with good reason: I wore glasses, I carried an armload of books, and my hemlines fell below my knees and not by choice. I was always either reading or heading to the library— or reading a book *and* heading to the library. People assumed I was destined to become a librarian.

And I was not very popular. I had one girlfriend and two "fans." Okay, they were not fans in the usual sense of the word, but these two boys did follow me around so that should count for something. I am sure they thought it funny to follow the weird girl around. Whenever I turned and caught them behind me, they would stop and point to something in the sky. I called them fans, but by today's standards we would probably call them stalkers.

The popular girls hung out together in large packs and surfed; I did not like putting my head in the water. The cool girls wore skirts so short you could see their bikini bottoms. With my below-the-knee-length dresses, I was a candidate for a convent.

My weird, loner image was not advantageous when it came to dealing with the bathroom girls. One girl I remember was Deborah (not her real name). She had a soft voice and bulky muscles. She could have easily made the football team if they had allowed girls to play. And I am not talking about the punter position.

Deborah and the other bathroom girls broke all the rules— they smoked, stole, cut class, and fought. But you could not avoid them. Sprawled out on the bathroom floor with their backs against the wall and books scattered nearby, you stepped over them or suffered the consequences. Often they puffed on a cigarette—eyeing you as you entered and watching you as you left. You never left your belongings unguarded.

I remember Deborah because she liked to toss out a remark or two as I gingerly stepped over her. This was her invitation to allow me to inspect her muscles close-up. I knew if I said anything or looked her in the eye, I would be accepting her invitation for hand-to-hand combat. And I would not have been successful. Naturally I took great care in walking into a bathroom during my four years in high school. I always wondered about Deborah and the others like her but never had the courage to talk to them to find out what their lives were like.

Did they have aspirations? They did not become cheerleaders. They did not make honor roll. They were not members of any committees or social clubs. I was not even sure if they graduated. No one believed they would amount to much in life. Without a doubt, they were not considered successful, unless you defined success as the ability to fight and protect your turf.

As for me, I could not fight or protect my turf; I could barely swim. Me—successful?

My entire high school life changed during my senior year after I participated in Hawaii's Junior Miss scholarship program. After winning, people saw me differently, even though I had not changed. I still wore glasses and carried around an armful of books, but people saw me as a "winner." The next thing I knew I was voted "most likely to succeed." My face was on the cover of our local newspaper—glasses and all. I am not sure what my classmates were thinking. Maybe they thought becoming a librarian was the epitome of success. But this accolade did not pave my way through life. It was not success, just positive recognition, and fleeting at that.

"Thank you for attending our reunion. And now we hope you'll take the time to get reacquainted." I looked around the ballroom for classmates I recognized. I had not seen many of them in a long time; my studies and work had kept me from returning to the islands for a number of years. A few surfer girls clustered together. Guys who had gained hair on their faces and lost it from their heads joked in the back.

One of the surfer girls, Roxanne, came up to me a few minutes later. We talked about our lives. She had married, had raised two kids, and had recently divorced. She did not surf, anymore.

As I conversed with Roxanne, I recognized someone across the room. She was dressed in a flowing ivory colored top and pants, but muscles still rippled beneath the fabric. She spotted me and marched straight toward me. Although I knew we were not in our high school bathroom, I felt every muscle in my body tense. Striding toward me, she was twenty feet away, then ten, now five. Suddenly she was within arm's reach. My mind blanked.

And then . . . she held out her hand to shake mine.

"Hello, my name is Deborah," she spoke in that same soft voice. "I'm not sure if you remember me, but I want to apologize for my behavior in high school."

I tried not to let my jaw drop as I nodded. I hope I thanked her for her apology and smiled. She turned and walked to another classmate and repeated her apology.

"Isn't Deborah amazing?" Roxanne asked.

"You mean her apology?"

"Yeah, but that's not all. Not only did she graduate from high school, she later attended college and got her master's degree. Now she works with troubled teenagers."

My jaw dropped again. Another shock. This time I had tears in my eyes.

That is when I thought about the meaning of success. It is not what you have achieved, but how far you have come. Deborah was not privileged; nothing in life had been handed to her. She literally had to fight for anything she could get. She did not have the same opportunities I had; no one thought she had any chance of making something of her life. But that did not stop her from reaching her goals. Now she was helping others who struggled with the same challenges she had faced, helping them to reach their potential. She had definitely come the farthest. If we could elect the classmate who had become the most successful, Deborah would get my vote.

Judge Leslie Ann Hayashi was Hawaii's Junior Miss in 1972. She graduated from Stanford University with Distinction in 1976 and received her Juris Doctor from Georgetown University Law Center in 1979. Leslie is an award-winning judge by day and author by night.

In 2003, the American Bar Association awarded Leslie the Franklin N. Flaschner Judicial Award, which recognizes the nation's outstanding judge in a court of special or limited jurisdiction. The "recipient must possess the high ideals, personal character and competence in performing judicial duties exemplified by the late Chief Justice Franklin N. Flaschner of the District Court of Massachusetts and shall have made significant contributions on local, state and national levels to continuing education of the judiciary and in other ways improved the quality of justice."

In 2005, Leslie was the first individual recipient of the Hawaii State Bar Association Outstanding Leadership, Diversity in the Legal Profession. This award recognizes efforts to promote diversity, equality, and access to the law. She is a faculty member at The National Judicial College in Reno, Nevada.

Judge Hayashi has also published six children's books: Fables from the Garden, Fables from the Sea, Fables from the Deep, Fables Beneath the Rainbow, Aloha `Oe: The Song Heard Around the World, *and* A Fishy Alphabet in Hawaii. *Her children's books have also received numerous awards (see* wwwfablesfromthefriends.com*).*

Leslie lives in Honolulu, Hawaii and is married to attorney Alan Van Etten. They have two sons, Justin and Taylor.

5

Happy with Me

Olivia Salter

As an elementary school counselor, I work with kindergarten through fifth grade students. At the beginning of the 2007 school year, I was asked by my principal to meet with all the children in my school who had "failed" their grade the previous school year. Oh! What a task! How in the world was I going to meet with these children and make them feel *happy* after failing their grade? After days of worrying about what I would say when I sat in front of these small human beings, I made a decision. I wouldn't focus on any "failures" that they had; rather, I would focus on where they were going.

I knew the children must already be feeling pretty down about repeating the same grade, while their friends moved on, so I made it my responsibility to help them move forward with a positive attitude. I helped each child to make two lists. The first list was of the things that they loved about their last school year and the happy memories that they had made. Most of them chose things like their friends, teachers, lunchtime, and playing outside. Then we made a list of the things that they didn't feel went so well and that they could do better, if given another chance. Almost all of their responses focused on struggling in specific subjects (like math or reading) and not getting good grades. When we sat and looked at their lists together, the children realized that in a strange way they had been given a gift. They could now repeat all of the things they loved from their previous school year (making new friends, going to PE, and playing outside), and they had been given a second chance to reach their goals from their second list. It wasn't about changing the past year, but moving forward to make things better. Through this process, I realized these children *wanted* to feel success. Perhaps not attaining their goal of passing their grade has given them the desire to achieve success.

Sometimes there are things that become so clear when we look through the eyes of a child. In trying to help these children, I reflected upon my own definition of success and how it has changed significantly over my 32 years of life. Growing up, I knew I wanted to be "successful," but what that really meant took years for me to understand. In elementary school success meant to get good grades so that my parents would be proud of me. In middle school, my definition of success changed to mean that I wanted to "fit in" with a certain group of kids. By the time I was in high school it evolved into wanting to make the cheerleading squad, so I could be considered by my peers as *successfully* popular. While I was always looking to find "success" I never felt like I had really figured it out. Through each experience I was growing and learning more about the person I wanted to be, but I always felt that the "next step" (whatever that was) would be the answer. So, when I got to college, I thought I had finally figured it out! All the hard work I had put into school was to help me become successful by having a good job that would help me make a lot of money. Then, I would find a man to marry and start a family of my own.

Now when I reflect on my life, where I have been and where I am now, I can more clearly define and understand what success means. It means to be happy with myself. Happy living in my own skin. Happy waking up in my own bed. Happy in the job I go to every day. Happy being me, and not wanting to be anyone else. *This was it!* The answer I had been searching for—my success was about my being happy with me!

So how did I get to this point? To be honest, I don't have a definite answer, but I do know that it was a series of experiences that helped me get to this point of being truly happy and feeling successful.

Taste Test

When I was a little girl, my mom signed me up for just about everything I could possibly do. I took gymnastics. I was a Girl Scout. I went to multiple summer camps. I took cooking and art classes. I swam on several different swim teams. I danced in a competitive dance company. When I was older and had the opportunity to be involved in school, I was in Student Government, National Honor Society, Vocational Honor Society, and many other clubs I cannot remember at this point in my life. The point is that even though I didn't love *everything* I was involved in (although I did learn to love almost all of it), being involved opened so many doors for me and my future. I encourage you to explore different activities and interests to find what you really enjoy. Find clubs, groups, and activities in your school and community to get involved in. Don't be afraid to "step outside of your box" and try something new. You will learn things that are fun, that you may have missed had you not tried.

Open Your Mind

Throughout my life I have met some truly amazing people, many of whom I may not have originally "chosen" to be friends with. Perhaps it was because they didn't look like me or live in a neighborhood like mine, but the more I was exposed to people who were different, the more I learned to value and respect those differences. I remember what it was like when I was in school, and I now see the same things when working with children in my school: people are grouped into categories. We often feel pressured to choose a group to be associated with. Should we be with the smart kids, the cool kids, or the athletic kids? The truth is, you don't have to choose! The world is filled with people of all kinds, and we can learn about ourselves from being open to meeting others. Why not be friends with them all and be the kid who is respectful of others? Let go of any ideas you may have had about someone before you ever met them. If you open your mind and learn to appreciate and respect others, you can learn so much about not only them, but you!

Stop Wishing, Start Living

When I was a little girl, I was always wishing for things to happen in my life. I wished I were a "big kid." I wished I were in middle school. I wished I had a later curfew. I wished I could drive a car. I wished I were in college. I wished I were married. *Wish, wish, wish!* Don't wish your life away. Enjoy every moment. You only get to live it once, and if you're always wishing for the next big thing, you'll miss all the little things along the way.

Live Without Regret

We all make mistakes. There are choices that we make without thinking twice, and sometimes things don't turn out as we had hoped. Sometimes we do our best at something and still don't get the result that we want. When I was in the 7th grade, I wanted to be a cheerleader, so I tried out. I didn't make it. I remember wondering, "What if I had practiced more? What if I had tumbled better? What if I had tried harder?" As I got older, I realized that all of those "what ifs" didn't help me. They only held me back from moving forward and trying something else. I was spending time and energy regretting things that I could not change. What a waste! I learned to live my life without having regrets. Use good judgment in the choices that you make, and do your best in all that you do. If you don't like the way your life is going, and you aren't reaching the goals you have set for yourself, change it! One of my favorite quotes that I often remind my students (and myself!) of is from Anthony Robbins, "If you do what you've always done, you'll get what you've always gotten." You make the choices in your life. Make them good ones.

Stop Comparing

Finally, I believe the most important thing to learn is also probably one of the hardest: how to love yourself. I know this was the case for me. There will always be someone who is smarter, someone who is a better dancer, someone who is prettier, or someone who is a faster runner. While it is wonderful to have people you admire, you cannot set your value or importance based on others. Your self-worth is not determined by how you compare with others. Learn to love yourself. Accept yourself for who you are, and respect your body, your soul, and your spirit. You are unique and special, just because you are you! The good news is that you will never be as good at being someone else as you are at being the one and only amazingly wonderful you!

Throughout the 2007/2008 school year, I continued to meet with those children who had "failed" their grade and watched them grow both academically and emotionally. I saw them make small steps to become better readers, make new friends, and eventually pass their grade. While I know they still have a long way to go, I value being able to help them to feel a bit of success. As I now reflect on those small human beings who sat in front of me sad and scared about repeating their grade, I once again realize how much these precious children have taught me. While it wasn't an easy journey for them, it was a necessary one. I am convinced that they learned something about themselves during that school year and that they will carry what they have learned with them to make their futures bright! Success is not an easy journey, as evidenced by mine, but it can be a fun one! It is your life, and it is what you make of it. If you can find true happiness within yourself, you will be a *success!*

Olivia Plymale Salter is originally from Cary, North Carolina. She earned her bachelor's degree in Elementary Education and master's degree in Counseling, both from East Carolina University. In 2004, she received her National Board Certification in School Counseling. Olivia currently works as the lead counselor at an elementary school, as well as a Master Teacher for an online reading module through the College of Education at East Carolina University in Greenville, North Carolina.

Olivia became involved in the Junior Miss program when she was selected as Cary/Apex's Junior Miss in 1993. Her love of Junior Miss led her to serve and give back by volunteering her time as a judge and committee member. She has served as the local chairman of the Pitt County Junior Miss scholarship program since 1999. In 2002, Olivia was named "Best Local Chairman" for the state of North Carolina. In 2005, she married Steve Salter and has two precious stepchildren whom she adores.

6

You Are Not What You Do

Jackie Rotman

I once had an article written about me in high school that started, "Jackie Rotman is every parent's dream child." By the end of high school, I had founded my own organization, Everybody Dance Now!, bringing free hip-hop dance classes to hundreds of underserved youth; I had achieved an impeccable transcript with straight A+s in 4 AP classes my entire junior year; I was captain of the Mock Trial team and earned perfect scores on my closing statement in the finals for the county competition; I was a leader in various clubs, community organizations, and choreographic productions; I was accepted to Stanford and Harvard and offered full-ride scholarships to other universities; and I was California's Junior Miss and 2nd Alternate to America's Junior Miss in 2008.

And then I got to college. For the first time, I felt like I was failing. Failing in my classes. Failing in my relationships. I felt like I was drowning—like everything around me was moving and I couldn't keep up, couldn't sleep, couldn't work, couldn't understand the things around me, couldn't find any sense of center or groundedness amidst all the changes. It was like I was lost in this huge ocean, and I didn't know who I was.

I kept wondering, "What happened to the girl who got A+s in every class, to whom failure wasn't an option, who could manage all her time booking it to the minute, who had her routine and her life together?"

At the same time I wanted to know what happened to that girl from my childhood pictures, who did cartwheels on the curb alongside the local pier, who ate chocolate popsicles with her dad and let the chocolate smear all over her face, who used bath soap with her brother to form beards pretending they were Santa Claus and Mrs. Claus, and who danced freely at a local festival wearing pink hair extensions, four-inch Rocketdog shoes, and a bright orange skirt and shirt? Who was that happy and carefree young girl staring back at me in a photo, crouching down on a field with her blonde hair down and a real smile?

Were those two people the same girl? Where were the intersections of the carefree young girl who glowed with life and the high school student who could succeed in various aspects of her life and achieve high goals? Was it possible for both to exist at the same time?

I had a realization that first quarter at college. I realized that for so long, I had defined myself by my accomplishments—California's Junior Miss, director of Everybody Dance Now!, the "Jackie Rotman" that people around town would talk about. When I was stripped of all that—my title, my organization, my community of people who had seen me grow up—and I was just me at college, I felt lost. I had been defined by my accomplishments for so long that I didn't know who I was without them.

That first quarter of college was a difficult time for me. I ended up having to go home from school that quarter and start again in January. But that time off from school and work was an amazing gift. That was a time of growth that enabled me to reflect on who I was and what kind of life I wanted to live. I had to grapple with the word, "success," and find out what it meant to me. And here's what I've discovered:

1. You are not what you do.

I used to think that people looked up to me because of my accomplishments or what I was able to do. At California's Junior Miss the summer I passed down my title and supported the next year's participants, I was a role model to many young women. The notes that the CJM participants wrote on a card to me at the end of our two weeks together were incredibly heartfelt and brought me to tears. But I'll never forget what one Junior Miss participant, Julia Berchtold, wrote: "I'm amazed by what you do but, more importantly, who you are."

I was surprised to read from all of these girls that the ways that I impacted them weren't just from what I was doing—like talking about various experiences, sharing advice or quotations, presenting about Be Your Best Self, or performing—or what I had done in the past; it was the times when I felt bad that I wasn't doing anything, except sitting in the room watching rehearsals and supporting the participants, that seemed to help these girls the most. Girls wrote to me, "I don't know what I would have done without you being there throughout all of our rehearsals and giving me energy to keep going." This showed me that there is essence beyond what we do, or what we've accomplished, that can bring joy to others and inspire them.

There's an essence in that little girl from my childhood photos that is powerful beyond any line on a résumé, any grade on a transcript, or any trophy on a wall. If we can tap into that essence of who we really are and channel that in our activities and endeavors, we will be well on our way to success.

2. Success comes from passion.

I truly believe that success comes from following your passions and doing the things you love. One of my best friends calls this "being faithful to Life." When I created Everybody Dance Now! and recruited a few other high school students to volunteer teaching dance classes to kids at low-income elementary schools, I did it because it was something I was passionate about and felt a calling in my heart to do. I had no idea how big Everybody Dance Now! would become and how many opportunities it would open up for me, as well as for the students I was trying to reach. For example, directing Everybody Dance Now! helped me to get into college, enabled me to meet other young leaders and win various community service awards, and even allowed me to be honored on America's Best Dance Crew's "ABDC Champions for Charity" episode in 2010. But I never expected or envisioned these benefits when I started the organization. Founding Everybody Dance Now! came from an innocent, intrinsic desire to do something I loved—to share the gift of dance with others. The other extrinsic indicators of success came later, on their own, because I was following my bliss.

On the other hand, with various endeavors in high school, I think that I sometimes got so wrapped up in trying to do them "successfully" that I forgot why I was doing them in the first place. A perfect example is our community's summer solstice parade. Every year since 8th grade, I organized a group of girls to dance in our local solstice parade at the start of each summer. We choreographed a dance, put together beautiful and elaborate costumes, and had an absolute blast dancing up the main street of Santa Barbara, connecting with people and sharing what we loved to do. It was our favorite day of the year, and we looked forward to it all year long.

But my last summer that I choreographed for the solstice parade—our 4th year—was a mess. I was stressed throughout all of the rehearsals, I was isolated from the group, and I had no energy to perform. The morning of the parade, I found out that all the girls had had a sleepover the night before, hadn't invited me, and spent the whole night talking badly about me and about how stressful I had made the solstice parade. They showed no appreciation for all the work I had put into preparing for the performance and helping us look great.

I later realized that the girls were right in a lot of ways. In trying so hard to make our group look good, I had forgotten the whole reason that I was doing the solstice parade in the first place: to have fun. After I realized this, I made a commitment to myself in my journal to "Live each day as if it were the summer solstice parade (the first three years we did it)." In other words, I was recommitted to pursuing my endeavors with a remembrance of why I started them in the first place—keeping in mind the pureness, passion, and love for why I was doing them.

I truly believe that if you follow your passions, you'll be so much more successful than you will be if you do the things that you think others will be impressed with or that will look good on your résumé. Last summer, I went to Uganda to conduct research on an educational nonprofit that teaches a leadership curriculum and mentors secondary school students to start initiatives that solve problems in their communities. My decision to spend the summer in Uganda was unconventional compared to other finance or corporate internships that many other sophomores in my position undertook, but I'm incredibly glad I did it. The 10 weeks I spent in Uganda were the best 10 weeks of my life, full of immense learning and growth.

Following your passions isn't always easy. It is sometimes at the expense of other safer options, can mean taking a road not traveled before, and can force us to draw on great strength and courage. But I believe 100% that passion leads to the greatest kind of "success" and happiness. I encourage young people to take risks to do the things they love—and parents to support them in doing so.

3. Success isn't defined externally.

All throughout high school, I worked incredibly hard to prepare to do my best at America's Junior Miss. Junior Miss pushed me to do my very best in school and various aspects of my life.

But during the entire finals night of America's Junior Miss, I felt like I was floating. Sometime after Friday night's show and before Saturday's finals, I stopped performing for the judges. Instead, I spoke and danced for my family and for every single person I met throughout my Junior Miss journey who believed in me—from my local and state committee members to my fellow Junior Miss participants and even some of their parents, from my host families to every volunteer I have met in this program. I performed for these people in gratitude and in celebration. And as I watched my friends express themselves on stage, I was able to feel proud of them and their growth, rather than compare myself to them. When the night was over, I remember feeling that nothing the emcees could read in the award envelopes would decrease or even increase the bliss, contentment, and pride that I already felt in my heart. I looked at the awards and medallions as merely one part of an experience with so much higher benefit.

And that's when I knew I'd learned what I needed to learn from this program. I had learned to believe in myself and rely on my strength in difficult situations. I had reached outside my comfort zone and gained confidence from overcoming my fears. I had pushed myself to perform much better than I could have imagined a year earlier, which empowered me and showed me that there are no limits if I work hard. Most importantly, I had stayed true to myself and had integrity—as well as fun! At the end of the day, it wasn't the achievement or the external recognition that brought me joy—it was the happiness and inner peace that I already had in my own heart because of how far I had come and what I had learned.

The week after I got home from AJM, I took my first yoga class in a long time. At the end of the class, the teacher read the second niyama in Patanjali's Yoga Sutras, which states that achievement and acquisition of things (whether it be mindstuff or materials) is irrelevant to finding inner peace. The only permanence in the face of change comes from within. This is the contentment that rests in knowing that our true nature, the unshakable Self, is our grace, compassion, freedom, and truth. We are already that which we seek.

It's wonderful to set goals, to dream big, and to work with perseverance and determination to achieve our goals. We should feel proud of ourselves anytime we put ourselves out there in this way. But we should recognize that the best judge of our success comes from within—not from anything that a judge or another subjective human being can ever tell you.

Moreover, we should never let the beauty of the present moment pass us by because we are too focused on what we want to accomplish in the future. If you spend your whole life in pursuit of goals, thinking that you'll find the happiness you're looking for once you achieve them, you're wrong. When I won California's Junior Miss in 2007, I expected to feel great for achieving this huge goal that I'd dreamed of for such a long time. But instead, I cried for days afterward, because in winning the competition, I felt that I'd become isolated from other girls in the program and didn't feel as happy as I'd expected. On the other hand, after America's Junior Miss, I was happy: I hadn't won the competition, but I'd formed incredible relationships with the participants, host families, and AJM staff, and had absolutely no regrets. It's the journey that counts—the value in each and every moment along the way. The joy we seek is in the present moment and in ourselves—not somewhere out in the future, when we've accomplished all of our goals (or not accomplished them).

I'm now in my junior year at Stanford University. I continue to work hard, and I have dreams of attending law and/or business school, pursuing a career that helps people in developing countries, and succeeding academically and in various fellowship/scholarship competitions that I am applying for. But I'm different than I was when I started college. I try to remember the three lessons I've described above (you are not what you do, follow your bliss, and success isn't defined externally) to make sure that I do what makes me happy and enables me to experience success the way that I define it. It's about working to achieve our goals not out of feverishness or a desire to please others or fit the mold that society sometimes encourages—but out of a place of authenticity, knowing who we are and drawing on our unique strengths and the powerful essence that comes from deep within us. How do we do this? I don't have all the answers, but I know that it takes continual recommitment, and it takes practice.

I now take an hour out of every day just for yoga and meditation to stay in tune with who I really am and what I feel. That clarity is the most important thing to me, because staying centered and maintaining a positive relationship with myself is where all the success begins. Life goes on externally: we win things, we lose things, we achieve goals, we fail, we love, we're rejected. But if we can find and maintain that strength within—that centeredness, love, and inner peace—we'll be able to get through any obstacles, to grow, and to be successful in life.

Jackie Rotman is a 19-year-old junior at Stanford University majoring in Public Policy. At age 14, Jackie founded Everybody Dance Now!, an organization which has provided free dance programs to over 1,000 underprivileged children in Santa Barbara, CA, and has inspired and supported chapters in 10 cities throughout the United States and Canada.

Jackie is passionate about issues of international development, education, cultivating leadership, and empowering youth. In 2010, Jackie lived in Uganda for 10 weeks, funded by a Stanford grant, to conduct research on a nonprofit called Educate! that teaches leadership and social entrepreneurship skills to Ugandan secondary school students. From 2009-2010, Jackie served as copresident of Right to Education for All Children (REACh) at Stanford, which cultivated partnerships with and raised over $6,000 for 3 schools in the developing world. Additionally, Jackie is the only college student who has been certified as an instructor for the Art of Living Foundation's Youth Empowerment Seminar! (YES!), a program that teaches yoga and meditation techniques to help young people successfully navigate through adolescence. Jackie spent time in India, where she participated in a Haas Impact Abroad trip with other Stanford students in 2009 and worked with a community NGO to create a school student council to help the village, and Guatemala, where she helped to organize her youth group's service trip in 2008.

Jackie was California's Junior Miss and 2nd Alternate to America's Junior Miss (now called Distinguished Young Women) in 2008. She thanks Distinguished Young Women for helping her to learn about herself, meet incredible friends, and develop into the strong young woman she is today. Jackie received a variety of scholarships that have helped to pay for her education, and she hopes to use her education to contribute to positive and sustainable social change.

7

Lifelong Learning

Rochelle Rosian, M.D.

I am Rochelle Rosian, M.D., a staff physician at the internationally known Cleveland Clinic, where I practice Rheumatology. I am the cochair of the Women's Professional Staff Association and an Advocate for the Arthritis Foundation. Professionally, I've worked very hard to have reached this level in my field, and I believe that success is about accomplishment, or overcoming challenges in order to reach goals. This starts with working hard in school, getting good grades, reevaluating your goals, and developing good habits.

The Encarta World English Dictionary's definition of success is "the achievement of something planned or attempted." My parents' definition of success is for their children to do better than they did. My concern is that many young people believe success is the "impressive achievement of fame, wealth, or power," as defined by the Oxford English dictionary. So given that I fall somewhere between my parents' generation and the youth of today, how do I impress upon you my definition of success in a way that's relevant?

It's rare that I get to sit down and list the accomplishments of which I'm most proud in my life, which include passing the American Red Cross Lifesaving course, dancing the part of Clara in *The Nutcracker*, making the freshman basketball team, and being chosen

1983 Ohio's Junior Miss. I am proud of my academic achievements of graduating from medical school, completing an Internal Medicine residency, securing a Rheumatology fellowship training position at the prestigious Cleveland Clinic (here's some perspective: only three out of 100 of us got the gig!), and passing the Internal Medicine and Rheumatology Boards. If you think that was the end of my education, I happily passed my recertification after 10 years, as well. The professional accomplishments are numerous, but I'm even more blessed in my personal ones, having found a fantastic life partner and having the fortune of three routine pregnancies and three healthy children. I have the benefit of a flexible work schedule, leadership opportunities for my professional development and growth, and opportunities to volunteer for the Arthritis Foundation and in my children's schools.

Perhaps this all sounds sweet and sunny, but it wouldn't be a complete picture if I didn't share the obstacles endured along the way. And as much as accomplishments define my success, overcoming these obstacles further defined me and what is important.

Some of the obstacles now seem trivial, but they were truly crushing in their individual moments. Not making cheerleading in the seventh grade, not playing basketball on the Junior Varsity team, and being an alternate for a six-year Bachelor of Science/M.D. Program at Northeastern Ohio University's College of Medicine were major hurdles at a tender age.

There were other disappointments, as well: I wasn't able to get into my first medical field of choice, dermatology, and I had a couple of failed relationships that damaged my fragile ego and peppered my personality as a young adult.

But getting through these rough spots of early adult life better prepared me for what lay ahead. Because I had experienced setbacks before, an emergency C-section and being passed for a promotion seemed like little bumps later in life that I could deal with because I was prepared.

True success is the ability, health, energy, love, and support to work toward our goals with drive and dedication. I like the line by the band U2 that says, "Ambition bites the nails of success." We must try new things to keep growing, but we must also balance our ambition with common sense and experience. On the quest for success, lifelong learning is a must.

Success is also being able to make contributions to improve and impact the future. Ponder the words of Albert Pike, who said, "What we have done for ourselves alone dies with us; what we have done for others and the world remains and is immortal." Living the Golden Rule of treating others as we would like to be treated and fostering a culture of mutual respect can help to build that kind of success that lasts beyond our lifetimes.

So am I successful? I'm not sure, yet. I am still working on my current goals of being a good wife and soul mate to my husband. I am working on being an excellent mother to my children. I am continually striving to be a caring and thoughtful physician to my patients. I aspire to be a role model to future physicians and patients alike. I work hard to be a good friend. My future goals are simple, really. I know there will be rough spots along the way, but with goals and dedication, there also lies the possibility of success.

> To laugh often and much; to win the respect of intelligent people and the affection of children; to earn the appreciation of honest critics and endure the betrayal of false friends; to appreciate beauty; to find the best in others; to leave the world a bit better, whether by a healthy child, a garden patch, or a redeemed social condition; to know even one life has breathed easier because you have lived. This is to have succeeded."
>
> —*Ralph Waldo Emerson*

Rochelle Rosian is a staff physician at the Cleveland Clinic in Cleveland, Ohio. She was chosen as Ohio's Junior Miss in 1983, and the scholarship she received from Junior Miss enabled her to attend Northeastern Ohio Universities College of Medicine, NEOUCOM. After completing an internal medicine residency, she completed her fellowship training in Rheumatology at the Cleveland Clinic, where she has been in clinical practice for the past 15 years.

Rochelle has been selected as Top Doc in Cleveland, as chosen by her peers and Best Doctors, Inc., since 2001. She was elected copresident of the Cleveland Clinic Women's Professional Staff Association and is also involved with the Arthritis Foundation. She is also involved in education, teaching medical students, residents, and continuing education courses in empathy in clinical practice.

Rochelle lives with her husband, Jon, and three wonderful children in Shaker Heights, Ohio.

Cultivating Success

8

Academic Success

Amy Osmond Cook, Ph.D.

One afternoon, my seven-year-old son bounced in the door after school, threw his backpack on the chair, and said, "When I grow up, I'm going to start a company that makes blocks. Then at night, I'm going to be an inventor."

"Sounds like a great idea," I said. "What are you going to invent?"

"I'm going to invent spy gear."

"Sounds cool. Now you have to do your homework."

"Aw, Mom. I don't want to do my homework."

"If you want to own a company and make spy gear someday, you have to do your homework." And the battle begins.

As a mother of four and an instructor of communication and interdisciplinary studies at Arizona State University, I understand the importance of achieving academic success. By this I mean not just getting good grades, but also looking ahead to get into the college or university you want to attend and doing well once you're there. In this chapter, I'm going to give you some tips that have helped me and others reach our academic goals.

Success is much more than academic achievement. Teenagers across the country have defined it as happiness, having goals, having a good job, having a family, following God's will, making good money, working hard, and being educated. For me, success is happiness, which comes from experiencing spiritual, mental, physical, and social fulfillment. But even though success is much more than doing well in school, academic achievement is connected to many areas of success. Achieving academically will help you get a good job, become an intelligent person, and make good money. It will also help you learn to achieve your goals and work hard. I know this has been drilled into your heads over and over again, but how do we actually get there?

In my many years of teaching, I have come across all types of students. Some are shy; some are outgoing. Some are quiet; others are loud. Some are lazy; some are hard working. Some are great students and some are not. What's the difference? From my experience, the A students do a few extra things that B and C students do not do, and that seems to make all the difference. Following is a list of the top ten things you can do to succeed academically.

1. Read the syllabus.

The very best thing you can do the first day of class is to read the syllabus, or the class instruction sheet. It is here that you find clues as to what the teacher likes, hates, wants, and doesn't want, as well as what assignments are due and how to do them. It's an easy enough thing to do, but it surprises me that so many people don't read it—and their grades suffer. For example, I've had at least seven people say to me this semester alone, "I didn't know we were supposed to turn in the assignment!" or "I didn't know when this was due!" It's obvious that they didn't read the instruction sheet or syllabus for the class. Some teachers will allow confused students to make up missed assignments, but most won't. I'm patient with my students, but I remember which students don't follow instructions and which ones do.

2. Research the teacher.

Remember the kid that got called a "brown-noser" because he tried a little too hard to flatter the teacher? His mistake wasn't that he was playing the teacher—he was just too obvious about it.

Teachers are just like anyone else. They have likes, dislikes, pet peeves, personalities, and preferences. When I say "play the teacher," I don't mean that you should try to butter her up for a good grade. Most people dislike false praise, and it will backfire on you. What I do mean is to find out what things your teacher really values. Is he a stickler for spelling? Does she like you to write in black pen? Does he hate it when people give excuses for why their homework is late? Find out what your teacher likes and dislikes and follow his or her preferences to a "T." Most of these can be found in a class syllabus or on assignment instructions. I write down all of my preferences in my class syllabus at the beginning of the semester. My biggest pet peeve is when students email me about an assignment they didn't "understand" when it's obvious they haven't read the assignment instructions.

This advice applies in other situations, too. Take Zac Efron, for example. This star of *High School Musical* decided to audition for one of the roles in *Hairspray*. He walked into the audition with long blond hair and a surfer look. The producers were looking for a slick 1950's-style look, not his. He didn't impress them and nearly blew the audition. As luck would have it, though, the producers decided to give Zac another shot. This time he came in with the right "look," and he got the part. Achieving academic success means not only working hard, but also finding out what the teacher is looking for.

3. Do all of your homework on time.

I once had a student named Dan (not his real name). Dan was an older student, what we'd call "nontraditional." He spent his early life as a chef, working for places like the Ritz Carlton Hotel. When he was 50, he decided to go back to school. This required him to take all kinds of classes in subjects he wasn't very familiar with, like mass media. Dan wasn't the best writer, and he got some of the answers wrong, but he didn't let it bother him. He did all of his homework on time and wrote long, detailed answers. He also took his homework one step further and tried to find ways that it applied to real life. He participated in discussions and asked other students questions. As a result, he learned a lot. As his teacher, I didn't care that he didn't get all of the answers "right." I was impressed with his dedication, and I found myself trying to find reasons to give him extra points.

Most teachers are like me. We decide to become teachers because we find it very fulfilling to help others learn. And when a student actually wants to learn, well, that's something to be excited about. Dan got an A because he worked hard, period. My guess is that you will, too, if you demonstrate to the teacher that you're going to do your best and are interested in learning. If you find yourself bored after school because you're doing your homework while others are out goofing around, just remember that a lot of other kids in America are doing their homework, too—and it will pay off.

4. Come to class.

Some students feel that as long as they do the assignments, they should be able to receive full credit. In reality, much of the learning that goes on in the class is a result of class discussion. In my political communication class, for example, most of the real learning takes place in class. The assignments give us theoretical tools to use, but the book is just a supplement to help us understand politics in real life. For example, right now we're trying to understand the 2008 presidential candidates and why they said what they did. None of that is in the book. You may think that class discussion is pointless (and in some cases, it may be, depending on how good the teacher is), but if you want a good grade in the class, you need to come to class.

5. Disagree strategically.

We all know bad teachers. Some are controlling, some are deadbeats, and some care only about the paycheck. Fortunately, these teachers are in the minority. Most teachers really care about their students and want them to succeed. For me, I get a feeling of intrinsic gratification when I see a student achieve success.

Whether your teacher is bad or good, there may be times when you disagree. At this time, it's important to remember that your teacher is in a position of power and you are not. It probably shouldn't be this way, but it is. Your teacher has some control over your future success, and whether he's right or wrong, he deserves your attention.

If you're in a situation where you and your teacher disagree, first evaluate what your teacher is saying and try to understand where she's coming from. Try to put yourself in her perspective and follow instructions. She might say something totally wrong like, "I don't think you put a lot of effort into this," or something you disagree with like, "You didn't use enough examples in your essay." See if you can understand what she's talking about. Next, respectfully state your position. Don't tell her she's wrong or incompetent (even if she is), or she'll get defensive. Say something like, "I thought that I used a lot of examples in my essay, like in paragraph two . . ." Then, listen to what she says. You might learn something you hadn't thought of before. Even if you don't, the fact that you're willing to listen and learn will give you brownie points. Finally, no matter the outcome of the exchange, thank her for her time and instruction and reiterate your desire to learn and work hard. Even if you lose the battle (maybe you want a grade change and you didn't get it), you'll probably win the war (she'll pay more attention to your work and, because you were respectful to her authority, she'll try hard to help you learn and get a good grade).

If a teacher ever degrades you as a person, of course you should defend yourself and perhaps even ask for intervention from the school. But more times than not, respectfully approaching a teacher with a desire to learn will get you ahead in the long run.

6. Don't be afraid to disagree with the teacher in a discussion.

Now, just to make myself clear, questioning how a teacher runs the class is *very* different than disagreeing with a teacher on a discussion question. One of the most important things students learn in college (and high school) is critical thinking skills, or how to think independently, analyze issues, and speak confidently and knowledgeably about a subject. One of the major objectives of most university (and other) teachers is to teach critical thinking skills. So, when a teacher poses a question in class, don't be afraid to answer it truthfully. Just make sure you have evidence to back up your claim. I, for one, am excited when a student disagrees with me in class and has evidence to back it up. It means that I'm doing my job teaching critical thinking skills.

7. Ask the teacher to explain.

I know it's hard to believe, but teachers do occasionally make mistakes! Once, when I was in high school, I got an A– in an English class. Now, an A– is not a bad grade, but I thought my scores reflected an A for the class. I went to the teacher and asked (respectfully) why I got an A– rather than an A. She looked at her grade book and said, "Oh, you should have an A. My husband was the one that filled in the bubbles for the final grade submissions, and he made a mistake." Needless to say, I was very glad that I asked!

Sometimes, I'll have a student ask me why he or she got a bad grade on an assignment. Last week, one of my students emailed me and said, "I was just wondering why I got 17/20 on my assignment, so I can do better next time." From this email, I knew she (1) was a good student that cared about her grade; (2) was a nice person because she asked me to explain in a way that was respectful, not accusing; and (3) wanted to learn. I emailed her back, thanked her for asking, and said, "Send me your assignment, and I'll look it over." It happened that her paper just wasn't detailed enough—something that she could fix easily. She has received full credit on her papers ever since! A good teacher will always appreciate an honest inquiry.

8. Be respectful to other students.

My goal as a teacher is to facilitate an environment where every student feels safe to voice his or her opinions and feelings. When one student makes fun of another, it makes it impossible for me to give students that safe environment. It makes me feel very good when a student writes on an evaluation, "My teacher respected all of my opinions and made me feel like I could actually say what I think!" If students are mean or degrade other students, even when they're just trying to be funny, teachers will NOT appreciate it, and your grade will suffer.

9. Never cheat.

This one goes without saying. If you get caught, there will be lasting consequences. At Arizona State University, where I teach, anyone caught cheating gets an XE on his or her transcript, which indicates that a student failed the class because of academic dishonesty. This designation stays on a student's permanent record, for all future employers to see. You DON'T want one of these. But even if you get away with it, cheating is probably one of the dumbest things you can do to yourself. By cheating, you're implicitly telling yourself that you're incapable of succeeding on your own merit and you're not worth spending time and effort on. You're also failing to teach yourself how to work hard and complete difficult tasks, both skills that you'll need to succeed in a career later on. You're worth more than that, so don't sell yourself short!

10. Never give up.

One bad grade means absolutely nothing to me as a teacher. I have had students do poorly on one assignment or test, decide to put effort into the class, and then snag an A by the end of the semester. I'll even sometimes let students redo their work, if they ask. I also grade on improvement. A B student that does consistent work throughout the semester will get a B. But a B student that takes my suggestions, applies them, and shows improvement will get at least a B+ and sometimes higher. Even if you're not the best student, showing improvement and working hard will get you further than you ever thought you could get!

In the end, grades do matter.

While academic success is only one area of success, it is connected to many areas of your life. Academic success will teach you valuable life lessons like perseverance and humility; it will also bolster your career and improve your self-esteem. It's never too late to start. If you're looking for a way to do better in school, make the choice now to improve your grades and follow the top ten things you can do to get a good grade. If you put forth the effort, you'll be happy with the results!

Amy Osmond Cook is a faculty associate in the School of Letters and Sciences at Arizona State University, where she teaches interdisciplinary and communication courses. She was America's Junior Miss in 1994 and is very grateful for the incredible experience and scholarship money that enabled her to receive her B.A. and M.A. in English from Brigham Young University. She later received her Ph.D. in Communication from the University of Utah.

As a violinist, Amy performed for multiple years with the Osmond Brothers. She released her debut album, Nativity *(a collection of traditional Christmas songs performed on the violin and harp), in 2004. She has taught violin lessons and worked as a freelance studio violinist for many years.*

Amy has been featured in print publications such as People Magazine *and* USA Today *and on television programs such as* Good Morning America.

Amy is married to Jeff Cook, and they are the proud parents of four beautiful children.

9

Success in Many Forms

Leah Kackley

What is success? Well, as you can see by all the wonderful stories in this book, success comes in many different packages. And it comes with many different faces, titles, and ideas. While I have yet another story to tell, I want you to take to heart one important idea: *Finding success starts with knowing who you are.* Let me explain.

The process of achieving success revolves around a consistent journey towards your goals. However, your goals must be defined by who you believe you are and who you believe you can be. For example, I think we all would agree that Carrie Underwood's pursuit of a career in music is a pretty smart choice for her. But could you see her as a professor at a law school? Either choice requires years of dedication and hard work, and both are considered successful careers, but Miss Underwood has a fire inside of her that is fueled by performing on a stage. And she has a God-given talent to sing. She is sure about who she is, and she is willing to do the work to continue along her already successful journey. Could she be a law professor? Maybe, maybe not. But even if she could, would she be passionate about it?

Let me tell you about my journey to the personal success that I found. I'll tell you about why I took the road that I did, and maybe you will see how it might relate to your experiences. I also want to give you some tools that you can use to help you identify what you feel passionate about. As you will see, this identification process is like the perfect GPS system in your car. As long as you fuel and care for your car, then that GPS system—knowing your passion—will guide you directly to your desired destination.

My Story

I spent my junior high and high school years involved in my classes. I also spent a lot of time involved in extracurricular activities. While I did have a good time with it all, I also did all this in an effort to hopefully secure a good scholarship to college. The hard work paid off with a full academic scholarship to Mississippi University for Women. And with the scholarship money I received through the Junior Miss program, each semester I registered meant the university wrote *me* a check. Can you believe it? But, my point is that my goal for the moment was to secure college scholarship money, because that was important to me. Knowing myself helped me to focus my attention, which in turn helped me to achieve this important goal.

Once I began college, I faced the decision about what my major should be. That's when I had to start analyzing what was really important to me, for the long-term. I had to figure out what I really wanted to do with my life. Let me tell you that at 17 or 18, that is a deep-thinking process. But, to me, that process is where the path to success begins. Knowing who you are. Knowing what fires you up. You know what? Sometimes the path to success begins with simply understanding that you haven't *yet* found that thing that ignites your passions. For me, though, I knew something about myself, even in my very early teenage years. I knew that if I was given the blessings of a husband and children, then I wanted to be a stay-at-home mom. I knew that no matter what career I pursued after college, raising my children would become my new profession when my first child entered the world. Knowing that was liberating, but I still needed to focus on an educational path to prepare myself for life after college.

After soul-searching and getting advice from trusted adults (specifically my parents), I felt a calling to become a teacher. I knew I loved the process of education. And I loved working with people. Teaching was an honorable and valued profession to pursue. However, at that time at MUW, one didn't major in "secondary education." I needed to decide on what major subject I wanted to focus, and then I would get my teaching credentials in addition to the degree. I finally majored in math, because I have always been drawn to that subject area. I got sidetracked, however, during my junior year of college, because I began working at the Engineering Research Center at Mississippi State University with the computational engineering and grid-generation group. Even though I didn't feel called to do this kind of work after college, it seemed more "important" than teaching. I got caught up in the possibilities of this exciting new field. The bottom line is that I lost my focus on my heart's desire and decided not to finish getting my teaching credentials. I finished my degree in math; but since I didn't have the burning desire that graduate school requires, I found myself in the business field, instead of the classroom. After spending some time in management at a rental car company and then at a mortgage company, I came back home to Brandon, Mississippi and began working for my father's consulting electrical engineering firm in Jackson, Mississippi. I helped with electrical design work and did some minor software programming.

During this time with the engineering firm, I met a most wonderful man who was also in the engineering industry. Jason's firm and mine were both designing a new convention center in North Mississippi. My firm was doing the electrical design, his firm was doing the mechanical design, and we met while working on that project. We were married in February of 2002, when I was 30 years old. We had our first child before we celebrated our second wedding anniversary—and when she was born, I became a stay-at-home mom. Our little Sarah was (and is!) full of joy and full of energy. And her arrival ushered in a change in my life and career. My passion had never changed—and that passion was to be at home with her, and later with our son, Noah, and our second daughter, Molly, in order to fulfill what I knew was my most important professional calling.

Like I mentioned before, I always knew deep down that when I had children, I would be a stay-at-home mom, no matter what career I was pursuing at the time. And I have always known that about myself. Even way back in high school when I was contemplating what in the world I should write down as my college major, I knew that eventually I would lay aside my career to be hands-on in raising my children. And, almost fifteen years after graduating from high school, I realized that goal of being at home with my child. But would you call me successful? If you measure success in terms of happiness and passion, yes! Knowing and understanding my passion helped me to make a decision that wasn't always strongly encouraged by society in general. And it also helped me to understand the importance of living a full and honorable life before the time came to be that mother.

Success is knowing exactly what is important to you and what impassions you. Read that sentence again. Knowing yourself in that way is no small thing at all. Being honest with yourself about your true goals and dreams is something that will keep your life moving steadily towards a future that will be filled with contentment, excitement, and true passion. Be aware, though, that hobbies and other interests may not necessarily be the passion you should follow. For example, I sincerely love the art and discipline of ballet. I have danced all my life. I have sweated away more hours in a ballet studio than I can remember. I have danced some memorable roles that will be treasured memories of mine for as long as I live. But, as much as I fantasized about dancing professionally, it wasn't what I knew I was supposed to do. I knew, because I quietly listened to my heart that ballet would forever be a part of my life, but it would not be my profession.

Achieving Your Own Dreams

As you involve yourself in activities at your school and in your community, you should honestly evaluate how those activities fire you up. Are athletics a chore? Or do you look forward to almost every practice? Is student government something you do just for your résumé? Or do you find yourself thinking about it when you wake up in the morning? Is volunteering at the children's hospital something you do just because your youth group from church does it? Or can you clearly see yourself as one of those doctors or nurses who continually works to find a cure?

This honest evaluation will help guide you in your decision making. When you get excited about an activity—for example, volunteering at a hospital—then think about what part of that activity moves you the most. If you find that talking to the patients is the part that engages your heart and mind the most, then you may be a nurse in the making. If you find yourself listening in on conversations between the staff and the business directors, then you may be a future accountant or business manager. If you find yourself wanting to know more about the conditions of patients, then you may need to start thinking about medical school. If you are most moved by the beauty of the flower arrangements that you deliver, then your true calling may be as an artist, or floral designer, or even a gift shop owner. Remember, our dear Sarah didn't come into this world until I was 32 years old. Even if in your heart of hearts you know that you want to be an at-home mother, then you may very well still need to pursue a fulfilling and honorable career until your wee one arrives. Your experiences will translate into gifts of knowledge for your family!

As you are evaluating your experiences and trying to listen to your heart and mind, be careful of comparing yourself with your friends. Not everyone is supposed to be interested in doing the same things. It's okay if your very best friend in the whole wide world is passionate about taking care of animals and you are passionate about teaching children to be excited about math. Your differing passions will mean quite different college and professional experiences. Your lives will be different, but you will always have the common ground of following your heart's desire, of being true to yourself. You shouldn't jump off of the "Veterinarian School Bridge" just because your best friend plans to put "DVM" behind her name.

There is something important that the decision to become a full-time mother has also taught me about success. True success isn't measured by money or fame or titles. Sometimes those things do come as a part of the journey. But if you feel drawn to a path for your life because of those things alone, then you will eventually find yourself floundering. You'll have difficulty feeling real excitement for what you do. And I would bet that you won't ever be able to say to yourself, "I am successful." Why? Because you'll always need more money or fame or better titles to continue to feel successful.

I know a true story about a man who was raised inside a life of literally royal circumstances. He had every advantage at his disposal; money, power, fame, and social connections could get him anything he wanted. He wanted for nothing and could have his craziest whim fulfilled. Seriously, he lived in such opulent circumstances that those rock stars on MTV could never even compete. If he had defined success as simply being rich, then all he had to do was to continue along the same path that he was already traveling. Yet, he knew himself to be God-made for a different life. He embraced what was in his heart instead of chasing the power and money that he could have had. He chose to leave the "easy" life and instead led a much more difficult and strenuous life. But, he also became a revered leader of a nation of people. We all know his name—Moses. His choice to follow the right path, instead of the one full of material gain, not only gave his life meaning and purpose, but also carved his name forever into history.

You will never hear me say that figuring yourself out is a super easy task. Most things of true value will not come easily. Nor will you hear admonishment from me, if it takes you longer than most to figure out how your talents and your goals should be blended with each other. Sometimes traveling slowly and surely can beat speeding down a road that ends with you being lost. But make no mistake—a successful person is one who finds the life path that God has intended for her and travels that path to the best of her ability. She will be quick to call her life happy.

Take charge of your happiness and success by taking time to notice what excites you. Don't compare yourself with your friends— imitating them might slow down your journey to success. Remember that money or power or fame is not an instant measure of success. Working for those things alone can throw off your focus. And, finally, being patient with yourself while you put the pieces together can help to keep you from making unwise decisions.

Realize your dream and do the planning and the work that it takes to follow that dream. Then you will be able to say that you truly have found your success!

Leah O'Gwynn Kackley was proud to serve as Mississippi's Junior Miss in 1989. She is a graduate of Northwest Rankin High School in Brandon, Mississippi and holds a Bachelor of Arts with honors in Mathematics, magna cum laude, *from Mississippi University for Women. At MUW, she was a member of the Lockheart Social Club and served as president her senior year. She was involved with many other organizations, including Interclub, Mortarboard, Hottentots, and Modeling Squad. She was also inducted into* Phi Kappa Phi.

Leah performed leading roles in a number of ballets, including Sleeping Beauty, Nutcracker, Graduation Ball, *and* Coppelia. *During college and in the years following, she taught both ballet and ballroom dance as a part-time instructor. She is an active member of Grace Primitive Baptist Church and is an executive member of the Board of Directors for the Rankin County Junior Miss Program, where she is a cochair of the production team. She also judges both local and state Junior Miss programs.*

Leah has been a full-time, stay-at-home mother since 2003. She has been married to her dearest friend, Jason, since 2002, and they are the proud parents of Sarah and Noah.

1 ●

Healthy Living

Tiffeny Thompson Crow

I realized one day that most people would like to set goals and have success towards healthy living, but they do little to accomplish their goals. I can give several examples. In college, I was writing a paper on goal setting. I was interviewing a girl at the Laundromat, and she exclaimed wholeheartedly that her goal was to lose weight. However during her explanation, she was feeding on a bag of potato chips. Fifteen years later, I heard the same thing as I sat around a table with a group of ladies who talked about their next diet and how they were all going to start "on Monday." As they talked, they were enjoying donuts and cookies. They asked me what was the best way to get healthy. I explained to them that they knew exactly what to do: Eat healthy and exercise. One said, "I just don't have the time" as she was enjoying a six-hour ladies' day out. She had the time; she just choose to use it in a different way. There are those who make excuses and those who take action. *You can be successful at healthy living*!

At the end of this year, I was asked if I had a New Year's resolution. I replied that it's a daily determination for me. When you set a goal of any kind, including success towards healthy living, that's not the end. You need to set for yourself smaller goals to help you accomplish the overall goal. Renew your mind every day toward your goals and go for it! If you slide off track, don't wait until Monday—just jump back on.

I've been an aerobics instructor for fifteen years. I love to exercise. It's a hobby. It's my passion. But I still have to set for myself goals on keeping physically fit. Even though I love it and it's my job, I get busy. Time passes. I get tired. There's too much going on. The excuse factor comes into play. I have to set for myself daily goals to stay on track for the bigger goal of staying healthy. At an early age I would set for myself goals towards healthy living. I would make charts and put them by my bed. I would check off a box for each glass of water I drank. The goal was eight glasses. I would check off boxes for how many laps I swam if it were summer, or how many blocks I walked. I even had goals towards doing so many jumping jacks or sit-ups. Now my goal list is much the same. I still keep my goal sheet by my bed. Before I get in bed, I need to have done one hundred sit-ups (various types of small crunches), one hundred arm exercises (push-ups, biceps with dumbbells, etc.), and one hundred leg exercises (such as lunges or squats). This targets most of my body in a short period of time each day. It takes less than 15 minutes if you go straight from one to the other. I use these steps to achieve my greater goal of healthy living.

For a healthy lifestyle, you need to include daily exercise of some sort. You need to include aerobic activity and weight training throughout the week. They both have fabulous benefits. Aerobic activity requires increased oxygen intake. Aerobic activity helps to control your weight or help you lose weight by using excess calories that otherwise would be stored as fat. Some examples are walking, jogging, an aerobic class, jumping rope, or dancing. Sometimes if it's hard for me to get in the mood of aerobic exercising, I just turn on the music and start dancing. My kids love it, too. For the weight training, you should be lifting enough weight so that when you finish your last repetition, it should be with difficulty but good form. While weight lifting, make sure you breathe and have good posture. A lot of times when it starts to hurt, we hold our breath. Keep breathing. Use control and good posture. Take your time.

There are so many ways to have success towards healthy living. I'll share a few fun ideas:

1. Snack smart.

Prepare healthy snacks so when you get the munchies, chips and cookies aren't the only quick grab. Buy the bag of small carrots already peeled and ready to go. Have any kind of your favorite raw vegetables on hand. A lot of fruits are bought ready to eat. Bananas and apples are great. I try to take a snack sack of some fruit or vegetable with me everywhere I go. When I get hungry, there's an automatic snack for me and my kids so we don't get the urge for fast food.

2. Keep a cup.

I keep a cup by my sink in the bathroom and by the sink in the kitchen. When I get ready in the morning, I consume my first glass of water. Every time I brush my hair or reapply lipstick, there's my cup, and I can take a quick drink, which can really add up. I keep one in the kitchen so I can readily have my water available as I'm doing my daily house duties.

3. Love the grocery game.

Always make your grocery list before you leave home. Check your calendar for the week and see what's ahead. If you're supposed to take something to a party or potluck, choose a healthy alternative. A cluster of beautiful grapes is always a hit. Check your list before you leave home. See how well you scored in making a healthy grocery list. I like to start with the fruits and vegetables. I tend to buy more when I start there because I know we need some snacks. If I start at the back of the grocery store where I come to the "snack" aisle first, I tend to get the unhealthy snacks. So the game is, when I'm ready to check out, I look at my purchases to see if I did healthy shopping. If I did, I won the game!

4. Crunch the commercials.

While watching a thirty-minute television show, use the commercial time to do some sit-ups, push-ups, squats, lunges, jumping jacks, etc. You'll be amazed at your workout. Make it a family affair. If you're in an activity during the commercials, you won't get caught "boredom snacking," which a lot of us do while watching television.

There are so many ways you can achieve success in healthy living. You know what to do. It's just doing it. Set those goals. Renew your mind daily. Make yourself a happy sign of encouragement to remind you of your goals. Tell yourself every morning when you wake, "I can be successful at healthy living." *You can*!

Tiffeny Thompson Crow was 1990 Arkansas's Junior Miss and the fitness and spirit winner at the national competition in Mobile, Alabama. While in Mobile, she also performed at a special dinner honoring the national judges and emcees. Tiffeny has enjoyed traveling throughout Arkansas and Louisiana judging, emceeing, entertaining, and choreographing several local and state programs.

Tiffeny toured with Up With People throughout the United States, Europe, and Canada and appeared on the Canadian Today Show. During her time with Up With People, she was named performer of the year.

In more recent years, Tiffeny has enjoyed traveling and speaking to various church and youth groups. She also serves as the president of the Ouachita Baptist University alumni board. Tiffeny has been involved in many church programs: She has coordinated the "40 Days of Purpose Campaign"; initiated an adopt-a-grandparent program; and sung with various praise teams.

Tiffeny has taught aerobics for 15 years and is currently AFAA certified. She helped to lead a fitness portion for children at the State Capitol for Governor Huckabee's "Fit for Life" campaign.

She's madly in love with her husband, Zac, and three children, Caleb, Isaac, and Lydia.

11

The Important Things

Jesika Henderson Harmon

All you have to do to find out what some people think about success is turn on the TV. There you will find people who will tell you that you have to be a certain kind of beautiful, have a certain kind of body, or have lots of money if you want to be successful. However, if you look in the homes and families of those who seem successful, you will not always find success or true happiness. I have seen and experienced that success does not come from money, fame, or the perfect body. Do you know where success comes from? True success only comes from true happiness. Let me show you.

When I was 21 years old, I traveled to the country of Zambia in Eastern Africa. There my sister and I spent a month teaching English in two different schools for orphaned children, volunteering in a Mother Theresa's Orphanage, and working in the neonatal ward of a hospital. I expected to get to Africa and see many starving, unhappy little children moping around. But surprisingly, I found just the opposite. Though most of the children I saw probably were hungry, you would never have known it as you watched them run around, smiling as they played with things like homemade balls made from plastic bags, sticks, and old tires. It didn't even phase them if they slipped and fell; with blood on their knees, they would brush it off and keep on playing. They were grateful for what they had. Success comes from how you deal with life. What do they always say: If life gives you lemons, make lemonade? It's true! Now perhaps many African people do not live in countries with successful governments or economies; most do not have good, high paying jobs; and many of them do not even have living parents. But the Africans I met are *doing what they can with the lives they have been given* and have found happiness in that.

Another experience that showed me what real success is was in my junior year of college when I interned for a United States Senator in Washington, DC. During my time there, I saw many "successful" people. But as I watched them and worked with them, I quickly noticed that so many of them seemed unhappy. The question arose in my mind, "Why aren't they happy? They have obtained highly competitive jobs, they make good money, and they are even well known by the public." I realized another key to success: *No matter how "successful" you are at work, you will never be happy unless you are successful at home.* Let me explain. The way we treat our families and friends is a huge part of who we are. Am I a good daughter, wife, mother, sister, friend? Most of the people I worked around did not have a husband or wife to go home to at night. Some had a spouse but were not planning on having children. A few did have a family at home, but they would stay late into the night doing "more important" work. You could see something was missing from their lives. I was fortunate to have a father who always showed us that family was first. He has a thriving financial management business and travels a lot. But he always made sure that we knew we were most important. He was at most every soccer game, dance concert, or piano recital cheering us on. We knew that he loved us because we saw that his work was never more important than we were. And though he is very successful in his business, his happiness comes from being with us!

I took a break from my college education to serve as a missionary for my church for 18 months in Hungary. Hungary is an Eastern European country that has only been out of communism for about 20 years. The majority of the population remembers what it was like to be oppressed and controlled, and many of them are still quite bitter about it. But while I was there, I met a woman who made a huge impact on me. Kati was a member of my church who was old enough to remember how awful communism was. However, she did not act bitter like many of the other older Hungarians I had met. She had suffered during communism as they had; and not only that, her husband had passed away years previously and she had a handicapped daughter. One day I asked her why she was so happy all the time when her life was so hard. She told me that *if you look for the good in any given situation, you will always be happier!* Kati was genuinely happy and content with her life, because no matter what came her way she found something positive about it. She had a good job, loving children, and faith that she stood by no matter what. When I thought about women I knew back home with husbands, money, great jobs, and beautiful healthy children, I could still think of more who were unhappy because they always dwelt on the negative. Kati was successful at overcoming the challenges life had presented her, because she chose to look for the good in her trials and found growth. And she was genuinely happy!

Perhaps you are thinking, "But how do I do that? How do I take control of my life?" Making the most out of what you have been given, fostering important relationships, and looking for the good in every situation takes practice! That is what life is: A chance to progress, a chance to learn from our mistakes, and a chance to ultimately become the best people we can be! Let's be honest, it is impossible to become a successful person without some pain. It's the journey that makes you who you are. And as you learn that *you* have control over making *your life* beautiful, the more successful you will be in whatever you do.

So how do I define success? Being grateful for what you have been given, focusing on family first, and looking for the good in every situation. Try it . . . you just might be closer to being successful than you think!

Jesika Henderson Harmon has been involved with the Junior Miss Program since she was chosen as America's Junior Miss in 2000. As AJM 2000, Jesika traveled extensively, performing dance, piano, and vocal solos along with promoting the AJM platform, Be Your Best Self. She has been a host and emcee for the AJM National preliminary and finals competitions for four years.

Jesika cohosted the Go For It *television program on the ABC Family Channel and has been a spokeswoman for healthy, happy living. Jesika has a strong belief in service and spent 18 months serving and teaching religion in Hungarian in Budapest, Hungary as a missionary for The Church of Jesus Christ of Latter-day Saints. She has been actively involved in other volunteer service, such as teaching English at the Bwafano Orphanage in Lusaka, Zambia; serving as grant writer and document designer for a nonprofit organization; working for the town of Chapel Hill's Resident Opportunity and Self-Sufficiency Program, which helps underprivileged women improve their health and self-image; and public speaking in various settings.*

Jesika graduated with honors from Brigham Young University, receiving a degree in English and Dance. While in college, Jesika performed as a featured soloist with the prestigious BYU Dancers' Company. While living in Chapel Hill, North Carolina, Jesika started a local Junior Miss Program and also volunteered as choreographer and judge throughout the state. She recently relocated to Arizona, where she serves as the chairman of Arizona's state program.

Above anything else, Jesika loves being a wife and mother. She currently resides in Mesa, Arizona with her husband, Robbie, four-year-old daughter, Bree, and two-year-old son, Gabe.

12

Success in Three Steps

Kim Lauren Schmidt

Goals. Determination. Personality. Those three traits have helped me achieve many things in life, such as being Rhode Island's Junior Miss 1983, Homecoming Queen for *Kappa Kappa Gamma* in my senior year of college, earning two master's degrees, being happily married for 13 years with three children, and achieving the rank of Lieutenant Colonel within the United States Air Force.

Goals

No matter what you would like to be or do for a career, writing down your goal can help. Then, you must decide what it is you need to do to achieve that goal. If you join the military (almost like Girl Scouts), these goals are already set out for you. To achieve rank, you must complete your appropriate training, have good performance reports, and move up with responsibility each year.

Sometimes your goals can change. When I entered the Air Force after graduate school as a Medical Service Corps officer, my goal was to achieve the rank of Colonel. That was before I got married, had three children, and realized that by achieving this goal, I would be putting myself above my family. To make the next rank, I would have to take a command at a base which the military dictated. My family would have to move (again). My husband probably would not be able to transfer his job within the government, and my children would have to make new friends and enter new schools. My goal of achieving rank has now changed to wanting to spend more time with my family. I have given almost 20 years of service to my country, and now I look forward to retirement to be able to take my daughters to dance, see more soccer games, etc. Goals change.

Determination

Do you have the determination to achieve your goal? All goals, from running for an office to losing 10 pounds to fit into those cute jeans to running a marathon, require determination to achieve them. Sometimes you may think you have checked all the boxes to achieve your goal but the decision is out of your hands. This is where determination can come into play. Maybe your goal is to get into the annual county holiday musical. My daughter, Erika, has tried out for this event three times and finally made it this year. She had to sing and dance. After the first tryout, we realized that she had a nice voice but needed some training to help build her confidence in singing in front of an audience. She used her allowance money to help pay for voice lessons and joined the church choir. Erika continued to improve in her dance classes and at last has made the chorus of the annual pageant. Her goal for next year is to earn one of the soloists' parts.

When I was 25, a female friend and I decided to climb the highest mountain in the lower 48 states: Mt. Whitney, in California. We had talked about climbing the mountain for 2 years, but various work and life-related activities kept us from actually making the hike. Finally, we just set a date on our calendar, packed our backpacks, drove to the base of the mountain, and started climbing to the top. We only passed one other woman on the way down the hill, which made us feel great. Although the trip to the top took us two days, it was so worth it to get there. Just like setting any goal, your hard work will pay off when you achieve what you set out to do. I look back and am so proud of my achievement!

There is a new book out that talks about the secret of success. The author says the law of attraction is one of the main secrets in life. Think positive thoughts, and your dreams will become reality. The book also discusses goals—they must be reasonable to be achievable. If you don't have the physical ability to reach the goal, you may need to change your direction, reassess the situation, and proceed from there. An Air Force pilot must have perfect vision. Many girls would like to be pilots, but if their vision isn't 20/20, they may need to be corporate pilots instead of military ones. These pilot candidates are not failures because they didn't reach the goal of becoming military pilots—they just must reassess their goals and change them slightly to fit into their physical abilities.

Personality

Your personality can either help or hinder your determination in achieving your goals. Know what kind of personality you have. Are you outgoing? Shy? Do you gossip? Are you scared of large groups? Learning about yourself will help you decide the right direction for yourself as you travel down the road of life. I would recommend taking the Myers-Briggs Type indicator to assess your personality type. It is available via the Myers-Briggs website. It was developed in the 1940s by a women and her mother to show people what type of personalities they have. They identified 16 distinctive personality types (extrovert/introvert, sensory/intuition, feeling/thinking, judging/perceiving), and from these classifications, you can really learn about your inner self and make obvious changes to overcome shortfalls.

When I entered college, I had a full ROTC scholarship. Since I was going to Virginia Tech, which still has a full-time military cadet body, I decided to turn the scholarship down. Virginia Tech was far from my home state of Rhode Island, and I didn't think the strict cadet lifestyle would fare well with my outgoing social lifestyle. I was probably correct with that thought since one of my bridesmaids, who was also a smart but social student, was kicked out of the program after a year for various rule-breaking. Of course, here I am with 18 years in the Air Force. My parents could have saved lots of money if I had taken the ROTC scholarship. But, maybe I never would have joined the Air Force. Who knows?

My biggest tip on how to improve your personality is to learn to become a good listener while being an interesting conversationalist. This means asking questions and listening with a caring face. I have run a 150+ member dinner club for years, and what I notice the most is that people love to talk about themselves. Many people can be wallflowers, but if you start asking them questions about their favorite sports team, a new movie, or even politics, they will come out of their shells. You never know if someone you strike up a conversation with can help you achieve your goal. Maybe your church youth minister went to the college that you'd like to attend, or perhaps he or she knows the coach of a team you would like to get on. Finally, if someone is speaking with you, make eye contact and mean it. I remember a friend who would be talking to me in the school cafeteria but was always looking over my shoulder to see who was coming in. Her body language said, "You're fine to talk to, but if someone better comes in, I'm going to eat at her table." Don't be that person. Give respect and true care to each conversation you engage in, and it will take you a long way in life!

Success. It means something different to all of us. To achieve my success, I set goals each Sunday morning before the kids are up, church starts, and the day gets in full swing. I try my hardest to achieve my goals using determination and my personality to help me along the way.

Kim Lauren Schmidt is serving as an Active Duty Lieutenant Colonel in the United States Air Force. She came into the service in 1990, right after graduate school. She has been a member of the Medical Service Corps (MSC) for the past eighteen years and serves as a Hospital Administrator for the 79th Medical Wing, Air Forces District of Washington, Andrews AFB, Maryland.

Kim was born in Cranston, Rhode Island and became Rhode Island's Junior Miss in 1983 while at Cranston East High School.

Kim double majored in Business and Broadcasting Communications at Virginia Tech. She was in the Kappa Kappa Gamma *Sorority (KKG Homecoming Queen 1987) and was Captain of the High Tech Dancers during her undergraduate years at VT. She also waitressed, taught ballet, rode horses, and worked in the library. Upon graduation in 1987, she sold life insurance for Southland Life and was named one of the Top 10 sellers in the county. Allstate Insurance offered her an office in Blacksburg, VA, but she turned it down to pursue a graduate degree in Management (also at VT).*

Much to her parents' chagrin, Kim decided to join the Air Force in 1990 and headed off to the Mojave Desert in Southern California. Her Air Force career has taken her many places: to Washington, DC, where she met her husband on a blind date; to England, where she gave birth to her first child, Karl; to Florida, where she and her family loved their annual Disney World passes; and back to Maryland, where she hopes to "retire" from the Air Force.

Kim has three children: Karl (11), Erika (8), and Stephanie (6). Kim is a Brownie leader, Girl Scout coordinator, PTA Chair, Room Mom, and Sunday school teacher. Her hobbies include meeting people, real estate, travel, wine, and selling Longaberger products since 1998.

Kim looks forward to the day when her daughters can participate in Distinguished Young Women.

13

You Gotta Be You

Patrice Gaunder Heeran

Success means making the world a better place because you were in it. Success starts with knowing who you are. Socrates said it best, thousands of years ago: "Know thyself." Until you know yourself, you will never discover what you have to offer to the world.

How do you know yourself? Self-knowledge involves so many things: learning, listening, studying, trying, doing, and making choices. It even includes making mistakes, learning a lesson, taking another road, and trying something else. Most importantly, self-knowledge comes through stopping every once in a while to rest and think and evaluate. Introspection takes time and yields important perspective.

Once you begin to know who you are and choose to live constructively, it really doesn't matter what you do. Author? Teacher? Actress? Doctor? Secretary? Homemaker? You can be and do many things *over time*. Ultimately, it doesn't matter to the "world" what you become. It has to matter to *you* and to those you hold most dear. Some of the most "successful" people in the world have been extremely unhappy and unfulfilled. Why? They were either living someone else's life (not their own) or gauging their "success" by the norms of the world (not their own). You get one life to live, and you must live it from the inside out.

Does that mean you wait until you "get it" to begin? No, there's the paradox: You can't know yourself until you start *doing* and making choices. Find what fits. What gives you joy, satisfaction, or a sense of contributing to the betterment of society? Do you have to make a huge splash? Do you have to be famous? Of course not. Very few people do or are. The huge majority of us matter only to a small circle of friends and family. Pick a path. If it doesn't work out, pick another one.

As America's Junior Miss, I wanted to set the world on fire. It was March 19, 1965. I was a 17-year-old high school senior and Michigan's Junior Miss. I stood onstage in Mobile, Alabama with 49 other state Junior Misses, all of us wearing our white formal gowns. The field had been narrowed to 12 semifinalists. Out of the 12, four runners-up were announced. That left eight of us standing there, wondering. My name had not been called. "Well, it's either everything or nothing," I thought. Then came the announcement that capped a year's worth of local, state, and national Junior Miss programs involving thousands of senior girls: "America's Junior Miss for 1965 is ... Michigan's Junior Miss, Patrice Gaunder!" The huge auditorium erupted in cheers and applause, especially my own fan club of some 50 classmates. They had held bake sales and car washes to rent a bus and follow me down to Mobile for the final night. This was the first year that the AJM program was televised: on NBC, nationwide, and in "living color." What excitement, what a thrill! That's me, I thought. My brief question of "all or nothing" had been answered: It was all.

I began to cry as the crown was placed on my head. Then I pulled myself together and took the walk down the ramp. My heart was filled with gratitude for the college scholarship I had just won. I returned to the stage and was greeted by my fellow Junior Misses. The TV cameras captured the crown tumbling off my head amidst hugs and tears and squeals all around. I was now representing all these wonderful, talented, intelligent young women as America's high school senior girl.

The year that followed was a whirlwind of new experiences and adventure: Touring some twenty major American cities, from Seattle and San Francisco to New York City, Denver, and New Orleans; doing interviews on radio and television and in newspapers and magazines, trying to spread the message of AJM; making commercials and doing fashion layouts in New York City; appearing at the Detroit Auto Show (Chevrolet was a national sponsor), the World's Fair, Broadway plays, and ballets; riding the AJM float in the Rose Parade in Pasadena; introducing the Senior Bowl Game live on TV in Mobile, Alabama; speaking to teenagers at appearances throughout the country; visiting sets and meeting famous actors like Little Joe (Michael Landon) of *Bonanza*, Myrna Loy, and Carol Burnett; and taking hundreds of pictures of my own (Kodak was another of our national sponsors). All of this was quite the heady experience for a midwestern girl who entered the AJM program in search of a scholarship and because it sounded like fun!

At that age, I wanted to do so much. I wanted to join the Peace Corps. I wanted to become a Special Ed teacher. I wanted to mold young minds. I wanted to change the world!

This year, I turned 60. I never joined the Peace Corps. I haven't changed the world. I used my $6,000 scholarship to attend a four-year liberal arts college for women, Marygrove College in Detroit. (Believe it or not, $6,000 paid for all four years!) At Marygrove, I learned to consider a subject from many perspectives: economically, historically, religiously, scientifically, even artistically. This perspective has served me well throughout life. Knowledge for the sake of knowledge is a wonderful thing. Learning how to think and reason is invaluable.

Graduating with a B.A. in English, I taught for a very short time. I then worked as a medical secretary, a full-time stay-at-home mother, and finally a church bookkeeper until my recent retirement. Deep down, I always knew my ultimate goal was to be a wife and mother. I knew I wanted children, and I wanted to raise them, myself.

During college, I met a wonderful young man and married him at age 22 (young by today's standards). We are still married after 37 years. My husband and I were blessed to bring three children into the world—all good, talented people and contributing members of society. There's a lot to be said for ripple effect. And I feel more serene, happy, and fulfilled than at any time in my younger life. Could that be "success?"

My generation said, "Never trust anyone over 30." Forget that. We were wrong. I've learned some "life lessons" along the way. You may find some of them helpful, if you don't mind trusting someone over 30:

- You are unique and special. So is everyone else.

- Know yourself. Accept yourself. Be yourself, your best self. You needn't become a CEO or a high-powered attorney. One of the greatest women I ever knew was a small-town hairdresser—deep, thoughtful, intelligent, funny, interested in others and in the world. You may not be the prettiest, thinnest, or smartest—that's ok. Aim to be *your* best and be kind to yourself. You have talents, abilities, and qualities unique to *you*. Develop them.

- Live in the present moment—not *for*, but *in*. Do whatever you're doing fully and with focus. Are you studying for an exam, waiting on a customer at McDonald's, driving your car? Be there fully. Focus. "Multitasking" is all the rage these days. I don't think it's possible. Something will suffer.

- Give of yourself and your talents. For me as a homemaker and stay-at-home mom, this meant not only baking cookies and getting my kids off to school on time. It also meant coaching soccer, teaching religion classes, volunteering in classrooms, serving on committees, participating in the political process, and serving as a Court Appointed Special Advocate for children.

- Find the positive—in people, in the weather, and in situations. If there is nothing positive, do your best to make it better.

- Read good books. Watch good movies. Listen to good music. Stay away from things that are negative or harmful. What you put into yourself, your mind, and your heart will come out in some way to affect your loved ones and the world. For good or for bad.

- Value down time. You cannot be going, doing, and achieving every minute. Take some time to just *be*. Sit quietly and allow yourself to savor life. Allow it to happen. This is important for children, too. Kids today are so programmed and scheduled that they have little time to explore their world on their own terms, or in their own time.

- Learn to listen. Be interested in others. Listening is a great gift to others, and you'll learn a lot, too.

- Aim for balance: emotional, social, physical, spiritual, and mental. Too much of one? Not enough of another? Sometimes you need more sleep, healthier food, more friendship time, or more alone time.

- Commitments. If marriage is in your future, choose a man you can talk to who has similar values about the important things like children, religion, money, and outlook. Discuss these with him. Date him long enough so you can see him in action. How does he treat his parents, siblings, and friends? How does he react to problems and crises? Is he dependable? Would he make a good father? Be sure you and he are a good match, because he won't change after marriage and neither will you.

- Children. If you opt for children, bring them into a stable, two-parent family. Children should not be an afterthought. If they are important enough to have, they are important enough to raise with your values, your time, and your love. Children are the most important decision and "career" you will ever have! The best nanny or daycare provider will never love or care about them as strongly as you will.

- Cultivate an attitude of gratitude, about everything. Meister Eckhart, a theologian of the Middle Ages, put it best: "If the only prayer we ever said were 'Thank you,' it would be enough."

Success is all about balance. Can you have it all? Possibly. But not all at once. Too many young women today want to have it all, do it all, and be it all, simultaneously. Be careful of this attitude: It's not all about *me* and my wants. You are here on this earth for such a short time. Make it count. Make the world a better place, in whatever big or small ways you can. Success is not about fame, looks, money, possessions, or talents. It's not necessarily about degrees or accomplishments, although many successful people have worked hard to attain those laudable things. Success is more about *who you are as a person* and *what you give* to the world. You don't need to be recognized or famous to be a success. You need to live *your* life, not someone else's—which is why it's so important to find out who you are and what you want to do or be. Maybe you will change the world. Or maybe you will quietly make a difference in your corner of it.

Patrice Gaunder was America's Junior Miss of 1965. She attended Marygrove College in Detroit, Michigan, graduating with a B.A. in English in 1969. She taught briefly before marrying John Heeran in 1970.

Patrice and John have lived in Chicago, Southern California, and Lake Tahoe, Nevada. They are the parents of two sons and one daughter, all grown. Patrice worked as a medical secretary until her oldest son's birth in 1975. For 20 years she was a full-time mom, volunteering in her church, schools, and community, including as a CASA (Court Appointed Special Advocate for Children).

She worked as a church bookkeeper from 1995 until her retirement in 2006. She and John currently live in Washoe Valley, Nevada.

14

The Spotlight Theory

Tyrenda Williams

I remember how frightened I was when the warmth in my tights and leotard signaled to my brain that I had indeed wet my pants. I was eight years old and surrounded in the dance studio by more than 30 members of the Alabama Ballet Company. I recall Sonia Arova, then artistic director, in her distinctive Slavic accent barking through her heavy smoker's coughs that I "come front and center to first position." Looking back, anyone could have assumed that she had demanded the Sugar Plum Fairy's variation from Act II from this frail, timid, and absolutely terrified forty-pounder. But, Madame Arova was merely comparing my height to the other seven children who had made the audition for the traveling troupe of Marshmallows in that year's performance of *The Nutcracker*. The truth and shame of the moment was that she made no demands. There was not a bit of dancing required or involved—nothing obvious that could have possibly incited so much fear in a human. The request was simply for me to stand, and to stand still. But my shyness and fear of being the center of attention had once again grabbed my senses and bodily functions. At eight years old, I recognized a feeling that I would never forget. It was this moment, though one of the most embarrassing, that would become my most prized and cherished memory of childhood. It was the moment I realized I was shy.

For most of my childhood I was very shy. I was almost painfully quiet, kept the same friends in elementary school, and much to my father's aggravation walked with my eyes focused only on the ground in front of me. At two and a half years old my parents decided for me that my struggle to become an extrovert would begin in the spotlight. I was enrolled in a local dance studio and would remain there for almost twenty years as both a student and teacher of jazz, tap, and ballet. It would be almost 15 years later when I finally realized how their plan succeeded and surpassed all expectation. From soaked britches at eight to the *Today Show's* green room with Matt Damon and Ben Affleck at eighteen, my life after high school began to unfold in ways I never could have hoped for as that shy and stage-frightened Marshmallow at the Alabama Ballet.

In High School I followed in my older sister's footsteps by joining the debate team. But unlike my eldest sister, Tycely, who excelled in oratory and individual events, I felt much safer in the realm of Lincoln-Douglas debate. The L.D.er's (Lincoln-Douglas) as they called themselves, spoke about reason and value premises and justice, and I wanted to know more about why and how these might be relevant to a teenager like me. Before I knew it I was speaking up more in classes, arguing more intelligently with my parents, and actually enjoying being called on to read in Sunday school. The first three years of high school were spent taking dance four nights a week, teaching three nights a week, and attending debate tournaments on the weekends.

During the summer of 1996 I entered a local scholarship program called the Jefferson County Junior Miss Program. It was well known in the Birmingham area for its generous scholarship awards, which many young women used to pay for college tuition. My ballet teacher thought I had a shot at winning the talent section and maybe a little money for college, so I entered and relied on my debate skills to get me through the rest. By the age of seventeen I noticed that when I got on stage to compete or perform in Junior Miss competitions,

I did not feel the way I felt that day at eight years old in front of Madam Arova at the Alabama Ballet. I think it was that the routine of performing in the spotlight began to get more and more familiar, enough to the point where I could simply say to myself, "Oh, it's just another rehearsal," or "Yep, just another debate round." In June of 1997 I was awarded the title of America's Junior Miss and began a year of extensive travel and appearances all across the United States.

At eighteen and as a full-time student at Birmingham-Southern College, I continued to make appearances in California, Utah, Rhode Island, New York, Georgia, North Carolina, Tennessee, and throughout the state of Alabama. It was truly an honor to represent my home state of Alabama and (though at the time I considered the following statement a "label") I was proud to be the first African-American to receive the title of America's Junior Miss. In September of that year I had the opportunity to appear on the *Today Show* (where I will admit to being more nervous about the two cute unknown actors in the green room—Ben Affleck and Matt Damon—than about my little blip on national television), spent an afternoon with Deborah Norville on the set of *Inside Edition*, and visited with Diane Sawyer at ABC News, where I would later intern with her at *Primetime, Live.*

As my year ended in June of 1998, I looked forward to a promising summer at ABC News; yet, I couldn't resist the chance to look back on the small steps that had been made to bring about such a change in my attitude, demeanor, and personality. Year by year I could identify some new outward expression of a new me developing. Whether it was beginning to talk more at the dinner table, or opening up my circle of friends through debate, or even taking on a job in a different part of town in Birmingham, I could sense an increasing confidence that drove me to desire the spotlight. I began to enjoy the challenges of being put on the spot and being pushed to uncomfortable limits, which gave me the simple satisfaction of knowing I had struggled before and had the potential to come out a winner. Do not be mislead, there were countless dance recitals between the ages of 2 ½ and 14 where I was frozen solid from the stage fright and horror of the spotlight. But as I have grown into my early twenties, completed my degree in Political Science, and traveled independently through France, Germany, Cuba, Mexico, Italy, Guatemala, Belize, and now Hungary, I step out into this world and discover that I begin to create my own types of spotlights. I have learned that it is in the spotlight that I thrive and excel, so it is here that I choose to be.

By no means is this "spotlight theory" of mine to be misunderstood as a complex where I crave to be the center of attention. (This is only the case when I and my two sisters and ten-year-old brother are in the same room.) Rather, I aim to find out how to benefit both others and myself as I confront any new challenges that arise. Success for me has always been the satisfaction of knowing that I had the potential to come out a winner.

Take for instance the year I served as a Guest Lecturer at Kodolanyi Janos College in Szekesfehervar, Hungary. Many people from the States have asked me, "What could a black girl from the Deep South possibly be looking for in Hungary?" And the answer is simple—a challenge. I was looking for a new type of spotlight and, fortunately, I found it. For most people in the town of Szekesfehervar, population 130,000, I am the first black person many of them have ever seen other than possibly on MTV or at sporting events like the European Basketball Leagues. I'll admit that it got awkward when perfect strangers ran their fingers through my curly hair or rubbed my skin to verify if it were indeed chocolate. One of my own college students asked me once if I tasted like a coconut! I've learned that these types of gestures then and throughout my life are motivated from the most innocent of curiosities, and I welcome these types of personal and real experiences. I learned that in one year I wasn't able to educate and inform an entire town in Hungary about life as an African-American in America and what it is like to be a young woman growing up in the South, who at times still struggles with inequality. But I will always be willing to open up or be in the spotlight to offer people a more real and accurate portrayal of the best parts of America and American culture for which I've been so fortunate to represent.

Tyrenda Williams currently serves as VP of Public Relations for LifeStageMedia, Inc. Her previous work experience includes Links of London, The Harry Walker Agency, GRID2, Ms. Foundation for Women, ABC News, and Kodolanyi Janos Foiskola in Hungary. Ms. Williams holds a master's degree in Journalism and Latin American and Caribbean Studies from New York University and a bachelor's degree in Political Science from Birmingham-Southern College.

In 1997, she became the first African-American to be named America's Junior Miss, the nation's largest scholarship program for high school senior girls.

15

Looking Back

Lori Jo Carbonneau

Maybe out of curiosity, or nostalgia, or perhaps in looking for a bit of a kickstart in writing this essay, I opened up an old AJM nationals program book. On page 9 of the 1987 America's Junior Miss National Program book, I found words written by an 18-year-old America's Junior Miss that remarkably ring true to me today. The Spirit of Junior Miss, it reads, is "a power which abounds in a girl who is confident of herself and is able to look for and share in the beauty and accomplishments of others." Hmmm, I thought, that's not far off. Today, were I to use that as a starting point for my definition of success, I'd make three edits. First, confidence in oneself is best when paired with courage to make a change when the situation doesn't meet your ideals. Second, "seeking the beauty and goodness in others" is actually an active commitment to building community wherever we find ourselves. Finally, we should view ourselves and our lives in perspective, knowing that each chapter of life brings a different embodiment of success—but what's constant is our own measure of ourselves.

You've guessed by now that I was that Junior Miss. And yes, with a few wisps of grey, or shall we call it silver, showing in my hair, I'm a bit nostalgic in rereading those words. It's remarkable, actually, that I found the program book, buried as it was in moving boxes from our recent relocation—home from several years living in Shanghai, China. So, what is it in these ensuing 20+ years that has made me amend my answer? And, more interesting, what has stayed the same?

A bit about these last 20 years: I've managed the operations of two different billion-dollar business; I've done an Internet start-up in the dot-com era; I've started my own businesses; and I've helped to turn around not-for-profit organizations. I've worked on Boards of Directors, I've quit jobs, and I've been fired. I've lived and worked in nine different U.S. cities, in London, and in Shanghai.

As you would imagine, success looked different in each of these chapters of life. In college and graduate school, success was generally about studying hard and doing well in my chosen extracurricular activities. In my early career, success was about admitting what I didn't know and seeking out opportunities to fill in the gaps. As a leader, surely it was about setting and meeting objectives—but more interestingly, it was about championing others. Back to the Spirit of Junior Miss: Be confident in yourself to the point you can seek out and champion others. Success in turning around organizations large and small doesn't come from sheer will. Rather, it comes from a group of individuals who share a common goal and are individually motivated to work together. I've found organizations were best motivated to work together when they believed that the leadership knew and cared about them as individuals. It's not too far of a stretch to see how my original definition of the Spirit of Junior Miss applies in each of these cases.

Act on Your Beliefs

So what's changed? I was a religion major in college, and I think I took for granted that all adults shared a common sense of morality. In one of my early jobs I learned differently. The president of our company asked me to fire two of my direct reports before their recent sales posted—so we didn't have to pay their full commission. Perhaps that was legal (though I doubt it); more importantly, I couldn't have looked myself in the mirror had I followed his instructions. But, I was junior in the organization, and he was the President. He said I was naïve. I honestly didn't know if I was, but I did have confidence those actions weren't ones I'd be proud of. So I quit—or maybe I was fired. It all happened so quickly we really won't ever know. But, I did learn an important early lesson: It isn't enough to have confidence in myself—success requires the courage to act in line with my views. It is important to remember that not only are we leading, but we are being led. Not only are we role models for others, but we're learning from mentors and are well advised to choose them carefully.

Look for the Beauty in Others

A few years later, I found myself sitting (rather nervously) with my classmates on our first day of our first year at Harvard Business School (HBS). HBS at the time had common vernacular around "hitting the screen." None of us knew how we learned that phrase, but we all knew what it meant: flunking out. At the time, our HBS class had about 800 students, and each class was divided into 9 sections of about 90 students each. In our section there were accountants, engineers, Ph.D.s, bankers, consultants, economists, and, yes, a Religion major. And each of us was individually daunted by the task ahead of us—to thrive—and whatever else happened, we didn't want to hit the screen. We knew what was to come: classes in finance and accounting, manufacturing and ethics, marketing and management, and my favorite, a humbly named class called "Business, Government, and the International Economy." Early on, I connected with a sectionmate named Dean. He had spent his early career as a Combat Engineer officer in the U.S. Army. Dean and I were similarly motivated—to not hit the screen and to make sure no one else did, either. Dean and I presented a plan to our sectionmates: as a group, let's be committed to no one hitting the screen. Let's do that by sharing our knowledge in subject areas we know and by seeking help in those we don't. Our class bankers held after school study sessions explaining Finance; our engineers shared their manufacturing knowledge; and so on. At the end of our first year, all 90 of us successfully moved on to our second year together. We were one of only two sections in all of our first-year class in which no one hit the scrreen. So, my suggestion to my 18-year-old self: not only is there reward in looking for the beauty (knowledge and) accomplishment in others, there is even more success that comes from actively building a community around the sum of your accomplishments.

Be Conscious of Time

The last edit I suggest to my 18-year-old self is to view life with a consciousness of time, seeing ourselves and our lives in perspective, and knowing that each chapter of life brings a different embodiment of success—but also knowing that what's constant is our own measure of ourselves. Indeed, each chapter of life brings a different set of challenges, joys, and victories. I never imagined that I'd feel the same rush from meeting a significant corporate milestone as I now do in hearing our 18-month-old acquire new language, seeing our 4-year-old begin to understand math, and watching the joy in our 6-year-old's eyes as his friends join him in games at his birthday party. I don't think I'd enjoy these moments as much as I do now had I not enjoyed individual successes in previous chapters of life. But, I do know that these successes look entirely different than the ones I'd grown accustomed to prior to motherhood. As I work my way through this chapter, I can't tell you that every day I don't feel a bit of a pull back to the familiar days of my business career—especially during those seemingly low-return activities like doing dishes and laundry. But I've come to understand that it's those mundane moments through these small but consistent acts that earns me the right to challenge my children, that gives me the quiet time to be near and hear them. And, I can state affirmatively, that these days with small children (despite feeling endless at some points) truly do go too fast. And, I do know that one of my life's most significant successes was having the confidence to kiss a lot of frogs while waiting to find and to marry the one who partners with me in parenting these little miracles. On days when my more public successes seem a long way away, it's he who reminds me that even after trading my business suits for play clothes, I'm still me—and who knows what other successes are yet to come. What will matter then, as it does now and always has, isn't what external measures of success are but how I feel about my choices.

One of the many reasons thousands of us are drawn towards the AJM community is the inspiration and energy we receive year after year from hearing the thoughts, learning from the insights, and experiencing the enthusiasm of young women. My goals of seeking out the beauty in others and celebrating the accomplishments of others aren't unique to me—rather, they are embodied by this community. When I look at the totality of the AJM community, just as when I reflect on the many directions the chapters of life have taken me, these themes ring remarkably true all these years later.

Lori Jo Carbonneau studied Religion at Princeton University and earned her Master's in Business Administration from Harvard. She was an executive at Bausch & Lomb in Rochester, NY and at Dell Computer in Austin, Texas. Additionally, she launched a start-up Internet company, which was acquired by CBS. Lori has been associated with McKinsey & Company in various ways since 1991—first as a consultant in the Atlanta and Washington, DC offices; next as a professional development specialist in Shanghai, China; and now as the wife of a Partner in the Washington, DC office. A recent professional and personal highlight was bringing Music Together, an early childhood music program, to Shanghai and orphanages throughout China. Other opportunities she values are building her teams and contributing to the growth of a variety of nonprofit organizations, including America's Junior Miss/Distinguished Young Women, the Atlanta Opera, and the Community Center of Shanghai. Currently, Lori is happily working harder than ever as the mother of three young children.

Lori counts her experiences as Virginia's and America's Junior Miss in 1986 and her continued associations with friends throughout the organization among her greatest blessings.

16

Standing Out

Katie McDermott

My parents have always pushed me to work hard in school and stay involved with activities that I am passionate about. When I came home with a ninety-six percent on a math test, I was always told, "Katie, if you had studied more, you would have stood out and achieved a one hundred percent." While as a young teenager this statement always made me cringe and silently bash my parents' thinking, I have now learned to thrive on it.

Being a teenager in a world filled with violence and a "know-it-all" media is difficult. Seeing drug dealers on television shows and celebrity failures on the news makes it hard for us to see that there are still good people left in our society. Finding and standing out as one of these life-changing people has become a mission of mine that I try to accomplish every day.

One lesson I have learned in both my schooling and extracurricular activities is to *never settle* for anything less than what you deserve. When working to obtain an A on a paper or a calculus assignment, use all of the resources available to you to ask for help. Letting the teacher know that you are a hard-working student will allow them to acknowledge your effort with a deserving grade.

When I was a senior in high school, I was in a class with my best friend who wasn't known to put effort into her work. My teacher assumed I was the same. When I received a B grade on my interim report, I emailed my teacher and let him know that I wasn't in class to fool around as he may have assumed. I wanted him to be aware that I was there to work hard and hand in acceptable assignments. Communicating with adults helps you to stand out as a respectable student in their minds.

Success in high school is vital, because it is an essential building block to your future, whether it is obtaining a college degree or heading into the work force. How is a young woman supposed to make an impression on a professor or an employer if there are thousands of others applying for the same spot? The answer is to simply *be your best self*. When writing an essay for a college application or interviewing with an employer, it is essential that you don't have a showy façade if that is not your personality. People can easily see through fake personalities especially if they have experience. Colleges and employers look for truly moral people to be part of their organization, and it is necessary that you are zealous about your goals to achieve this position. Find a way to express your enthusiasm by telling an employer that you will dedicate one hundred percent of your energy to your work because this is a position that inspires you, or write an essay on a topic that is meaningful to you.

Applying to college is a stressful process because it involves a great deal of time and energy, and choosing an essay topic is the main element of the application. As a junior I was struggling to pick a topic for my own college essay. I had spent many hours writing countless papers that had no feeling or meaning behind them and were not going to be acceptable for my essay. I finally decided on a sensitive topic that truly had meaning for me. I had to put my dog to sleep just weeks before, and it was a difficult subject, but it allowed me to put my heart and true personality into the essay. I was descriptive and emotional throughout the essay, and it was my way of reaching my readers and hopefully standing out to them.

Not everything in life is about standing out academically. It is vital to become involved in activities that you are enthusiastic about, such as the arts or sports teams. Trying out for a sports team or fine arts performance takes a lot of confidence. The key to earning a position is to *make a statement*. Even if you are not the most fit, talented, or art-savvy person auditioning, you should be sure to stay disciplined and practice on and off the field. Always ask questions if you are unsure about something not being done correctly, because people respect intelligent questions. It means that you are paying attention and truly have an interest in what is being expected for auditions or tryouts.

The dance program at my local studio is very competitive, and of course everybody wants to earn a position in the top class. When I was a sophomore, I felt like I was ready to perform with the "older girls." I called the owner of the studio and told her that I was ready to move up a level. She said, "Katie, you can go to the first class and see if the instructor thinks you are ready." After working through the first exercise, I was already intimidated by my fellow dancers' abilities. I worked hard the first few weeks and practiced routines on my own. My instructor didn't think I was ready, but I told her that I would devote all of my effort to dance and get extra help if needed. She reluctantly allowed my attendance in the class—and by performance time I had improved so substantially that I was named jazz student of the year.

Success comes in many different forms. It can be personal success in reaching goals or academic success in getting accepted to a university. By going beyond what is expected of you and thoroughly communicating your ideas and feelings, you will make an impression. Never settling for less than you deserve, making a statement for what you believe, and being your best self every day is the perfect recipe for standing out among your peers. Remember that it is crucial to diligently prepare for your goals so that you will never achieve less than one hundred percent.

Katie McDermott is a sophomore at Virginia Polytechnic Institute and State University. She is currently pursuing a degree in Business Management with a minor in Global Business and Chemistry.

Katie is involved with Sigma Kappa Sorority at Virginia Tech and holds the position of Junior Panhellenic Delegate. This requires her to attend weekly meetings with girls from all other Greek chapters and help to plan the Greek events on campus.

In addition to being involved with Greek life, Katie participates in Virginia Tech's Relay for Life. Last year, she was a team capitan, which involved putting together a team and raising money for the fight against cancer. Katie's other activities include being a notetaker for students with disabilites, participating in Virginia Tech's Leadership Program, and working with the Virginia Tech Women's Center.

Katie loves being a part of the Hokie Nation.

Katie has a younger sister, Maggie, a younger brother, Joe, and two extremely supportive parents, Denny and Fran McDermott. She currently lives in Chesterfield, Virginia.

17

Artist, Bride, and Imperfect Pot

Anne Hagerman Wilcox

I sat down on the piano bench and looked up at my vibrant music teacher of 10 years. She said, "I understand you have been chosen to attend the American Legion Auxiliary's Girls State event at Idaho's capital."

I was very excited to participate in something carefully designed to help young women understand government. Girls from all over the state of Idaho would be going to the capital for a week to act as representatives, senators, and justices. As always, my piano teacher had encouragement to give: "Well, I hope you run for governor. Someone needs to do it—and you would be so successful in that responsibility."

I was stunned. I had no thought of running for anything while being there, much less governor. I was simply excited to be going. As usual, she challenged my expectations. Exceptional teachers are like that. I could hardly keep my mind on Chopin. Run for governor? Why not?

A few short weeks later, 200 fellow 17-year-olds elected me as their leader, the Governor of Idaho's Girls State for 1971. As I sat that week in the Governor's office waiting to sign Girls State legislation, I realized I had experienced success because someone believed in me and encouraged me to try for dreams beyond my own.

Many years later in the summer of 2007, I was invited to go back to Idaho's Girls State and speak at the Inauguration. As I prepared, I realized it had been 36 years since I had occupied the Governor's office. During those years, I had had many opportunities to look more deeply at what true success is. I learned that success is only rarely defined by the winning of an election or the triumph in a contest. It runs much deeper than that. If I were asked to portray the truly successful person, my answer would not be a definition but rather a series of stories. I've loved stories all my life, from the early childhood fairy stories read to me by my parents to the intricate fantasy volumes of J.R.R. Tolkien in *Lord of the Rings*. The challenges encountered by the characters, the hope despite all odds, and the wonder of staying true to one's convictions even in the face of evil have always moved me. Therefore, I feel that although definitions of success are noteworthy, stories stay with us forever.

The following three stories and experiences have sustained me through difficult times and have given me a truer definition of success than any experience of winning. Together as a threesome, they provide key characteristics of the truly successful life. The first two stories are true, and the last one is a folktale. Each story in sequence portrays the nobility, the friendship, and the awareness of individuality needed for a truly successful life.

The first true story begins with a young orphan from Mexico. He had been adopted by Jewish parents in the United States. When I became his teacher, he was speaking in Spanish during unguarded moments, working hard on English during academic moments, and exploring the wonders of Hebrew after school at his synagogue. Three languages were going on in his head, and many times he retreated to what I thought was doodling on his school papers. During one history session, I marched over to his desk to stop the doodling and to redirect him to the lesson. Thank goodness something stopped me. There he was using the ovoid and u-form artistic techniques of the Pacific Coastal Indians to create beautiful animal drawings. I had introduced this art form as a supplement to the history lesson, but he was captivated by it. That's when I discovered that David's true "mother tongue" which could bridge all three languages was art. I began to let him represent his knowledge of our fifth-grade academic material through his drawings. He was understanding so much more than I had realized and seemed relieved to have a way to share his knowledge with me.

Finally, I invited a friend who was a professional artist to visit my class. Jim Lamb came with a deep understanding of art and a deep understanding of children, since he had three of his own. He enjoyed a discussion with my students, and then he began to draw. David was invited to come up close and help him. This insightful professional artist quietly gave David the English words for the tools needed for the charcoal medium being used that day. David was almost shaking with excitement as a large puppy took shape on the paper, perfect in form and detail—looking as if it would yap any minute.

After class, Jim stayed to look at some of David's drawings and to meet his parents. He then invited me and David's family to join him at his Gallery Opening in our city that weekend. None of us needed to think twice. We began to plan our trip to a real gallery featuring an artist now known to us all.

That weekend, as we piled into the car, I couldn't help but be amazed at the nobility of this professional artist who would share his "big moment" with an eleven-year-old boy. And I was about to find out that Jim had even more in mind than I realized.

When we arrived in back of the gallery, Jim was waiting and asked David's parents if David could "hang out" with him for a while. After receiving a "yes," Jim ushered David into the gallery. I snuck into a corner where I could watch them. I assumed Jim would be showing David his paintings and giving him some pointers. He did do some of that, but he did something even more incredible. Amidst the sophisticated event, Jim introduced David to his prestigious colleagues with these words, "This is my friend, David. He is also an artist." By these few words, Jim proved he was not only a successful artist— he was also a noble person. His actions revealed his belief that true success meant deeply encouraging the success of another.

The second story is also true. It happened on the night before a wedding. The bride was my daughter, and she had asked to spend the night before her wedding with me alone. We sat on twin beds in the upstairs bedroom of a dear friend. The two of us shared precious memories of the wedding week—a shower put on by good friends, a dinner with the groom's delightful mother, the bachelorette party, dinner on the water with the groom's family, meaningful moments from the rehearsal and the rehearsal dinner. Finally, we decided we'd better get some rest to be ready for the big day tomorrow. Before we went to sleep, I pulled out a small gift that expressed my maternal desire to always cherish this special bride and give her wings to fly at the same time.

Then my daughter surprised me by pulling a rectangular box out from behind her back. I smiled. It was the same kind of box she had handed to all her bridesmaids at the rehearsal dinner. In the boxes were beautifully etched, Lenox vases. "Oh," I said. "You got one for yourself. How nice."

"No, Mom. I got these for all my best friends."

"I just think that was so thoughtful—and your bridesmaids are some of the most incredible friends any person could have."

"No, Mom. I got these for all my best friends."

"I guess I don't understand."

"Well, I handed them to all my best friends—except for one. There is one best friend left to hand this to." She reached over and gave me the vase.

Nothing in this world—certainly no achievement—could ever mean what that moment meant to me. What a privilege to be a best friend to my daughter.

No one can be successful alone. In other words, the truly successful person is rich in friendship. Achievement without healthy relationships leaves one very empty. Therefore, the genuinely successful person must add to nobility a winsome ability to befriend others— just like this bride honored the friendships with her bridesmaids and her mother the night before she would commit herself to a lifelong friendship with a husband.

We've explored nobility through a gallery opening, and we've watched the importance of friendship from the night before a wedding. Now it is time for a third story which explores individuality. This traditional Indian folktale is about a cracked pot.

A water bearer in India had two large pots he would carry on a rod across his shoulders. One pot was absolutely perfect; one pot had a crack in it. The perfect pot always brought a full pot of water back to the home of the master. The pot with the crack lost half of the water on the way home from the well. The pot with the crack was discouraged and ashamed of his imperfection. He simply didn't feel successful in doing what he had been made to do.

Finally the cracked pot spoke to the water bearer and apologized for making the work more difficult for everyone. The water bearer just smiled and told the pot to notice the beautiful flowers along the path to the master's house. The pot noticed them but didn't understand.

The water bearer explained that he knew all about the crack in the pot. He said that he had planted seeds along the path so the water that fell out of the crack could feed the seeds and help lovely flowers grow. The bearer had used the flowers to decorate the master's table. He reassured the pot that without the "imperfection" of the crack, the master would not have had such beauty to enrich his days.

The successful person looks honestly at her weaknesses. Through this tale, we catch a new glimpse of the unique gift of our individuality as we express both our strengths and our weaknesses. A truly successful woman makes peace with her imperfections. Just as the cracked pot yielded beautiful flowers to grace the master's table, so each one of us through our weaknesses—not just our strengths—will also make unique contributions to our world.

These three stories—of nobility, friendship, and individuality—sustain us through the ups and downs of a competitive culture. Accomplishments, like being elected Governor of Girls State, come and go. Definitions of success also ebb and flow with the latest symbol of affluence. These stories, however, mature our perceptions in a world

often wearied by counterfeit fame. They compel us to express and
enjoy a deeper and more authentic success.

*Anne Hagerman Wilcox is the New Language Director for
the Wendell School District in southern Idaho. She had the privilege of
becoming Idaho's Junior Miss in 1972 and was a finalist at the national
level. Anne lived in the Northwest cities of Portland and Seattle for almost
30 years and grew as a teacher through a variety of experiences at the
university, secondary, and elementary levels of education. The highlight of
Anne's career came while instructing other teachers about the* Chronicles of
Narnia *during a C.S. Lewis Summer Institute at Oxford and Cambridge
Universities in England. The highlight of Anne's personal life has been the
delight of being the mother of Jaime Wilcox Staehle.*

18

If at First You DO Succeed . . .

Carol Buckland

For me, success is a state of mind. It's also intensely personal. Sure, many of us use external things—grades, awards, bank balances, job titles, newspaper headlines, etc.—to gauge if we're successful and, if we decide that we are, to measure how our level of success compares with other people's. But when push comes to shove, I believe that the ultimate determination of whether or not you're a "success" must come from inside you. It's a matter of you being honest with yourself about what you truly want to do with your life and how you want to go about doing it.

In the course of my career as a journalist, I've spoken with plenty of people who possess all the external trappings of success. Many have unabashedly declared themselves to be thrilled and fulfilled. They've described to me in vivid detail how they've dreamed big . . . and done even better.

While I've found myself inspired by some of these self-proclaimed successes (and, frankly, a bit repulsed by a few others), I've always been more interested in the apparently fortunate folks who've admitted to me that in their heads and their hearts, they feel like failures. They may be making millions and be flatteringly featured on the covers of glossy magazines, but they are desolate because in their pursuit of "success" they've lost track of themselves. They've neglected or abandoned their families. They've neglected or abandoned their friends. They've neglected or abandoned their core beliefs. No matter that they're perceived by the rest of the world as having it all. They see themselves as having little or nothing of true value.

I, personally, spent a long time defining my own success— or lack of it—almost entirely in terms of material "stuff" and other people's opinions. It worked pretty well, too, as long as I didn't listen to the little voice inside me that kept asking: "If this is success, why aren't you celebrating? Why don't you feel better about yourself and what you've done?"

While I wish I could share with you a single, dramatic incident that transformed my personal definition of success and my formula for trying to achieve it, I can't. I've never really been the "light bulb" moment type of girl. When it comes to mastering life's lessons, I've always been somewhat of a slow learner. I'm prone to needing refresher courses, too.

Let's just say that as much as I tried to soundproof my "successful" self against it, that nagging little voice gradually got through. And once it did, it goaded me into examining a lot of my assumptions about myself and my life. It also made me start remembering.

One of the most significant things I found myself remembering was how— years before—I'd responded to "success" in connection with my involvement with the America's Junior Miss program.

A few things you need to know about the teenage me: I was a grind and a geek. I was about as athletic as a rock of Jell-O. I hardly ever dated.

While I wasn't a pariah, I wasn't exactly popular, either. Which, looking back, wasn't a surprise. I didn't really like myself. If I'd had a choice, I probably wouldn't have hung around me very much.

I was also overweight. By how much, I can't (won't) recall. And don't go looking for old photographs. Except for one or two my brother may be holding in reserve for blackmail purposes (kidding!), they've all been tracked down and destroyed. I will, however, confess that there was a period when my nickname was "Carol the Barrel."

So, what happened? And what does it have to do with my perspective on success?

Well, to make a long story short, I read about the Junior Miss program in a teen magazine early in my high school career. I hadn't really heard much about the program before then. But the article—I think the article was titled something along the lines of "Smile, Sparkle, Be Yourself!"—hooked me. Frankly, I wasn't too sure about the smiling and sparkling part. But the "be yourself" exhortation struck a very powerful chord.

As it happened, the state in which I lived did not have local Junior Miss competitions. Instead, there was a Sunday afternoon mass "cattle call" during which JM wannabes were interviewed and assessed. Fifteen or so "finalists" were then selected to take part in the state program.

Inspired by the magazine article, I set a goal for myself. That goal was to become "worthy" of being one of the at-large finalists in the 1970 Connecticut's Junior Miss program. While my determination of what would make me worthy included using my brains and being attractive, it mostly had to do with trying to become comfortable in my own skin.

I didn't think about winning at state. I never once dreamed of taking home the national title.

In pursuit of my goal, I slimmed down and shaped up. I stopped focusing solely on getting straight A's and began participating in extracurricular, community, and church activities. I worked on developing my "people skills." I also took risks—reaching out beyond my comfort zone. I worked hard. I made changes in my life. I made changes in *me*.

I should add here that I kept my efforts a secret for a long time. This was partly because I was afraid that I was going to fail. It also had to do with my concern for other people's opinions. While *I* thought getting involved in Junior Miss was a good idea for me, I had serious doubts whether anyone else would. And, given my vulnerability to what other people thought about me, I didn't want to be dissuaded from my goal before I really started striving to reach it.

When they first found out that I wanted to enter a program like Junior Miss, my parents were shocked. They were worried that by involving myself in something so utterly out of character, I was going to be hurt or humiliated. In the end, though, they were very supportive of me. They also became completely sold on Junior Miss and its ideals. As for how the other students at school reacted when they discovered what I was up to . . .

What can I tell you? Even *after* I patiently explained that Junior Miss did *not* include a swimsuit competition and emphasized scholastic achievement and interviews, most of them thought it was a big joke. The incredulity I heard in my friends' voices when they asked, "*You're* going to be in a *beauty pageant*? Are you *kidding* me?" still resonates in my memory.

It's hard to describe the *"I did it!!!"* thrill of success I felt when my name was called as one of the at-large finalists for the 1970 Connecticut's Junior Miss program. The rush was so powerful, I nearly passed out.

I won't try to tell you that what followed—being selected as Connecticut's Junior Miss and becoming first runner-up to America's Junior Miss—wasn't wonderful. It was. I will always be deeply grateful for the friends I made, the opportunities I was given, and the scholarship money I won.

But it was all gravy.

Remember that little voice I wrote about earlier? Well, after a lot of reflection, I'm persuaded that one of the reasons I did as well as I did in the Junior Miss program was that I allowed myself to wholeheartedly celebrate the efforts I'd made and the success that had resulted from it. And in celebrating, I embraced the moment and let me be me.

Being yourself, your authentic self, is the key to success. While this may sound like the simplest formula in the world, it's not. Because to "be yourself," you've got to figure out who you really, truly are—and whether that's the kind of person you really, truly want to spend your life being. *You've* got to look deep inside and be absolutely honest about what you find.

Sometimes, you're going to like what you see and you're going to want to build on it. Other times, the view isn't going to be as nice. In fact, it may seem pretty ugly to you. But don't turn away! What you don't like about yourself, *you* can change.

As I've worked to discover and develop my authentic self—and let me emphasize, it's still a work in progress!—I've come to define success in a very broad way. For me, being successful involves doing my best in every endeavor and balancing the personal, professional, and spiritual aspects of my life.

When I say "doing my best," I don't necessarily mean finishing first or winning the grand prize. There have been plenty of times that my best has been pretty lousy in comparison with other people's efforts or achievements. But I can honestly say that I've reached a stage in my life where I sometimes feel more "successful" when I try my best and fall flat on my face than when I accomplish something through a half-hearted effort.

Several years ago, I was fortunate enough to be selected for a fellowship that allowed me to spend two months living and studying in Japan. It was one of the most exciting and educational experiences of my life. Among the many things I learned during my stay was the phrase, "*gambatte kudasai.*" It's something the Japanese say to you when you're about to start doing something.

While there's an element of wishing somebody "good luck" when you bid them "*gambatte kudasai,*" my Japanese friends have explained to me that the truer meaning is, "Please keep going and do your best!"

Please keep going and do your best.

If you embrace your authentic self and follow that admonition, I believe you'll be well on the road to achieving success in every facet of your life ... provided you keep one additional truth in mind.

As crucial as it is to figure out your own definition of success, it's only half the equation. You also need to determine what you're willing to pay to achieve it. Success may enrich and empower you, but it doesn't come free. It can cost you in blood, sweat, tears, time, energy, fun, friends, and family. Whether you can pay the bill—and still be your authentic self—is something only you can decide.

It's also something you need to consider *before* you start trying to achieve whatever your definition of success is. Remember my earlier mention of the people who judge themselves to be losers in life even though the world calls them winners? Well, very few of them consciously set out to screw up their families, sacrifice their friends, or sell their very souls in pursuit of fame, fortune, or first-place finishes. Most of them had no clue about the kind of tab they were running up until it was too late.

Don't be like them. Don't end up with a little voice telling you, "If this is success, it's not worth it!"

There's one other thing I'd like to share with you. It may not be something you want to hear, but it needs to be said.

Failure is an option.

No, it's not an option many of us would choose in our lives, but it *does* happen. And when it does, whether you treat it as an obstacle or an opportunity can be key to determining whether you get stuck in a nonproductive rut or motivated to move forward onto a positive path. One of my beefs with "self-help" literature is that a lot of it seems to advocate ignoring the possibility of failure. *No negative thoughts!* readers are ordered. *Negative thoughts breed negative outcomes! Envision success! Conceive . . . and achieve!*

That's all very well and good. And perhaps a relentlessly positive approach works for some people. But it's been my experience that refusing to contemplate the possibility of failure and to prepare for it usually means ending up in the creek without a paddle. Sometimes literally.

Think about it. Probably the ultimate "failure" for the captain and crew of an ocean liner would be having their ship sink in the middle of a voyage. But do they set sail without life boats, life jackets, and a carefully considered evacuation plan? I think not! And would you want to book a cruise with them if they did?

But that's *different*, I can hear you saying. No. That's reality. That's *life*. It's a journey. And even if you're optimistic enough to believe you'll never need it—and blessed enough to have this upbeat outlook validated by decades of experience—it's smart to travel with all the emotional, spiritual, physical, and financial survival gear you can carry. Smarter still to be ready and willing to use it!

Now, I'm not suggesting that the secret to success is surrendering to failure.

Heck, no! You surrender, you stop. You stop, you're stuck. Failure doesn't get the final word in your life *unless you allow it to*. Regard failure as an impassible roadblock, and it will halt you dead in your tracks. Look at it as a speed bump (they have a purpose, you know!) or a detour sign (you'll be amazed what you'll discover when you deviate from your meticulously mapped-out route), and it can become something extraordinarily instructive.

That's why I advocate that you treat failure—or "temporarily deferred goal accomplishment," as a friend of mine prefers to call it—as another part of the process of achieving success. When you set a goal, don't limit yourself to visualizing achieving it. Visualize falling short, too, and figure out what you'll do if that happens. Come up with a back-up plan! And a back-up to your back-up.

A friend of mine—you'd know her name if I mentioned it—says her motto is: "Prepare for the worst, and you'll almost always be pleasantly surprised."

Makes sense to me! Especially if you pair it up with the spirit of *gambatte kudasai*.

As I've mentioned, my career as a journalist has given me the opportunity to meet and speak with a lot of successful people. One thing I've discovered is that many of them experienced some kind of failure—professional and/or personal—early in their lives. None of them enjoyed it. But every single one of them overcame it. And by overcoming it, their fear of *future* failure lessened. They were liberated by the knowledge that if they fell flat on their faces again, they had the guts and grace to get up and keep going.

Oddly enough, early, unalloyed success can be a prelude to long-term disaster. It's a rare individual who can maintain his or her equilibrium in the intoxicating rush of grabbing the gold ring on the first try. That's because as soon as you succeed at just about anything, you're going to start feeling pressure to do it again, only bigger and better. And the possibility of failing to grab a second gold ring—or, worse, of losing hold of the one you've already got—can be utterly terrifying. It can paralyze you. It can eat away at who you are and leave little more than a scared, empty, has-been.

Failure isn't your friend. It isn't your enemy, either. But it can be a terrific teacher, if you have the courage to face up to it and learn.

Finally, when you succeed by doing your best as your authentic self—and I know you will—share the good fortune. Give back. Pay it forward. Lend a helping hand. You'll be better for it, and so will the world.

Carol Buckland is a veteran of the broadcast news business. She currently is the Senior Editorial Producer for CNN's award-winning Larry King Live. *She is also the author of more than two dozen contemporary romance novels published under the pseudonym Carole Buck. Carol is honored to have been Connecticut's Junior Miss and first runner-up to America's Junior Miss in 1970.*

19

Balance

Sally Spaulding

I have always had a passion for travel, but the itch to escape was never stronger than when I was growing up in a suburb outside of Birmingham, Alabama. While Birmingham is a large city by most standards, in my mind it just didn't compare with the global hubs that offered the best in culture, art, music, and theater.

Alabama seemed boring to me. Anything that could be labeled remotely "Southern" was automatically discounted in my book. I preferred classical piano to banjo and tried to speak without the twang that plagued my speech. I became a vegetarian to avoid eating the meat-infused vegetables and fried goodies that filled our family table. Rather than embracing the cultural idiosyncrasies that make the South unique, I pushed them away and replaced them with dreams of attending college in faraway cities that seemed so exotic and exciting compared to my own life in the South.

New York. Chicago. London. I didn't care. I was going to break away from my home. Completely shed my southern accent. Become some fabulous caricature of a cosmopolitan diva in a booming metropolis.

After winning my county's Junior Miss program and coming in first runner-up at Alabama's Junior Miss in 1999, I had the scholarship money to help make my escape become a reality. I enrolled in Wellesley College just outside of Boston, Massachusetts, and I began adulthood as I thought it should be.

While at Wellesley, the world opened to me. I landed a summer internship with the United Nations in Costa Rica and was able to study abroad my junior year in London and South Africa. I wrote for the student newspaper, reviewing plays, ballets, and symphonies. My academics were successful, and I even took a work-study position in the college's career office so I could get a glimpse of all the job opportunities before any of my classmates. Everything was on track for my high-powered, suit-wearing job in the Big City.

But the curveball of an economic downturn and a harrowing year for young graduates left me flustered. I wasn't landing the big public relations or publishing jobs that I expected. In fact, none of my classmates seemed to be getting hired. Should I go to graduate school and wait out the job market? Dejected and embarrassed, I took off the graduation cap and gown and drove home to Alabama.

For three months I sent out résumés for any job that looked interesting—and some to jobs that didn't look interesting at all. Eventually it was a suggestion from my sister, whose college roommate had a father in the newspaper business, to apply to work as a copy editor in Grand Junction, Colorado. I convinced the paper I was worth the risk and moved out to Colorado within a few weeks ... once I took a look at a map and figured out where Grand Junction was actually located.

The town didn't even have a decent mall. It was four hours to the nearest real airport, and actual tumbleweeds would dance through town on windy afternoons. I remember sitting in my little apartment, wishing I had some of that fried Southern comfort food and wondering how my life could have gone so terribly wrong. I had planned everything. I had worked so hard to make myself a success. How could I have failed so miserably?

I have never been more wrong. After working a few months as a copy editor, I was named the paper's environment and natural resources reporter and spent my days detailing the energy boom that had recently hit western Colorado, along with chasing fires and ambulances like most young journalists. Whether I was crawling down uranium mines, running after wild horses in the desert, or flying in small planes over wilderness areas to capture a story, each day was an adventure. Business suits certainly didn't fit with the job, and I regularly kept hiking boots at my desk just in case a story required them. Somehow in the midst of pursuing professional satisfaction as a reporter, I discovered a "nature girl" deep in my heart with one outdoor experience leading to another.

From learning to snowboard to rafting down the Colorado River, my time away from work became more exciting to me than breaking news stories. I soon realized my personal life had taken a front seat, and suddenly the constant night and weekend shifts of a reporting lifestyle didn't seem as appealing. Neither did the idea of living in a place with lights, pollution, and tons of people—a virtual requirement if I chose to climb the journalism career ladder and move to a larger circulation market.

The solution was easy when I was offered a job in public relations with the U.S. Forest Service's White River National Forest. The position allowed me to communicate stories and information to the public, a passion of mine, without having to sacrifice my life outside of work to the journalism gods. While I am no longer with the Forest Service, I have found a wonderful new home working as the director of public and media relations for the city of Aspen.

My success here is about balance. It's about working hard and then taking a few ski runs on a lunch break or simply soaking in the beauty of the mountains while walking to a meeting. It's about having the freedom to take a vacation to visit my family in Alabama and get a good ole' dose of those Southern roots I now appreciate and embrace.

If you told me any of this while I was plotting my big-city future, I wouldn't have believed you. "What, me? Rock climbing? *Right*," I would balk. "I could never do that." Now I simply smile at my younger self and tell me to follow my dreams of the moment, but always, *always*, be open to the unexpected ones that surface along the way.

Born and raised in Birmingham, Alabama, Sally was named Jefferson County's Junior Miss and was first runner-up at Alabama's Junior Miss in 1999. In 2003, she received a bachelor's degree in English and Environmental Studies from Wellesley College.

Sally is currently the director of community and media relations for the city of Aspen. Professionally, she spends her time involving citizens in their local government, producing and hosting a television show called City Matters, *serving on the board of Sister Cities International, and acting as the city's spokesperson in local and national media. Personally, Sally spends her free time snowboarding on one of the four local mountains, finding new places to explore in the backcountry, and performing at local venues with her jazz band.*

20

Ten Criteria for Success

Linda Delbridge, Ph.D.

Success can mean many things to many people—after all, we're all different. But I've discovered a few secrets that might help an up-and-comer like you. As a businesswoman, I hope I bring a unique perspective to the idea of success; but, you might be surprised that the principles I've applied in the corporate world can also lead to great success and happiness in life!

1. Dream big.
2. Set goals.
3. Be your best self.
4. Have a positive attitude.
5. Continuously learn.
6. Work hard.
7. Have faith.
8. Develop your character.
9. Innovate.
10. Marry the right person.

For some people, this list may seem obvious; but believe me, if you don't think about this early on in life, you can lose many years, floundering about and not really getting anywhere. One day, you may look at your life and think, "Is that all there is?" Many will have regrets of time lost, youth lost, or opportunity lost. "Shoulda, coulda, woulda" indicates a lack of understanding as to how one got there in the first place. I vowed never to use them in discussion, arguments, or other communication, since it is backward-looking and unconstructive. So take a look at this list, see what parts strike a chord with you and your life situation, and take them to heart. It's a list that works for someone who wants to become a businesswoman, a politician, CEO of a household (a.k.a., stay-at-home mom), doctor, teacher, nurse—just not someone who expects everything to be handed to her on a silver platter.

I've usually felt that most sayings, idioms, or expressions are somewhat tongue-in-cheek, old-fashioned, or just plain common sense. Some of you, like me, might even find then "corny." But, as it turns out, most are very pithy and speak to my heart, besides being easily remembered. So, in thinking about how to best respond to my definition of success, these phrases really resonated with me. Here's why:

1. Dream big.

Bless Diane Sawyer's heart (AJM 1963 and *60 Minutes* anchor). She delivered the baccalaureate address for the AJM National Program in 1983, its 25th anniversary. Her number one message for us was to "dream big." She is a wonderful speaker, and her advice spoke directly to me. It was so inspiring to see one of our own Junior Misses so very successful, yet so down-to-earth and supportive without really knowing any of us. To keep me motivated, I keep a picture of the 20 AJMs who attended nationals that year in my office to remind me of her inspirational speech and to always "dream big."

2. Set goals.

My mom used to tell me (and this was back in the 1960's before we had reached the moon), that I could be anything I wanted to be—even an astronaut—even though there were no women in the space program, yet. But we didn't have the financial assets to put three kids through college, so what was I going to do? Scholarships were the only option for me. Excellent grades, determination, and thinking differently led me to several scholarship opportunities along the way. They included scholarships from Junior Miss, Navy ROTC, the GI Bill, and IBM and culminated in my Ph.D. in Computer Science. All of this came without financial impact on my family. I attended the universities of my choice; I selected the fields of study that fit my skills, talents, and interests; and I have subsequently reaped the benefits of this education in my personal and professional life. One way in which I attained this educational success was to develop and record my short- and long-term goals, make a plan, and then check things off as they became reality. So set goals—what do you want to do today, this week, this year, this decade, in life? Write them down and you will discover that, as Les Brown states, if you "shoot for the moon, and miss, you will still be among the stars."

3. Be your best self.

It may seem trite, but adhering to the Junior Miss motto of "be your best self" is one of the best recommendations I have ever received. Since the Junior Miss organization formalized this program, it's become a wonderful testament to raising self-esteem in young people and motivating all of us to strive to be and to do our very best. Here's my take on the five aspects of the AJM Be Your Best Self Program.

Be healthy. In any kind of work, whether it be in school, your job, your family, or parenting, there is no one better to look after you than you. Don't forget the basics—be sure to eat healthy, get eight hours of sleep, drink lots of water, and exercise. Commit to being drug- and smoke-free. Also, be sure to take time out for yourself, even if it is only a few minutes every day. Where work is concerned, be sure to take all of your vacation at your job—your company will be happy to "use you up" if you don't and, quite frankly, you are a better employee when you are relaxed and at your best. Personally, I like to take a few quiet moments to have a cup of tea and read the latest technical or fluff magazine or take our two Alaskan Malamutes on a trail hike in the most beautiful place on earth: Lake Tahoe.

Be involved. Caring about your fellow man or woman and giving back according to your own gifts and talents is extremely uplifting and satisfying. Give it a try. Be unselfish and help others—it comes back to you tenfold. For instance, it seems like being a "good neighbor" is becoming a lost concept. Last summer, I organized our neighbors to get their properties at Lake Tahoe more wildfire-safe by coordinating an effort to help us remove overgrown vegetation, trim tree branches away from houses, and chip, not burn, the "slash piles." Also, recycling your trash can be someone else's treasure, especially in a sagging economy—so clean out that closet and help both yourself and others in need.

Be studious. Try to learn underlying concepts and principles; don't just memorize. Assimilating the concepts gives you a lifelong understanding of the subject and also imparts the ability to use that knowledge in everyday life, to "think on your feet." Studies show that high school graduates have an average income higher than that of nongraduates, and college graduates have an even higher average income, so you will reap the benefits of staying in school and continuing your formal education.

Be ambitious. You are here on this planet for a reason. You are unique and have talents that no one else has. In order to achieve your dreams, think about what you like to do and set goals. Find a mentor and be a mentor to others as you progress in your career.

Be responsible. The world is not always fair, and it certainly doesn't owe you anything. So make no excuses for where you are at the moment, and don't blame anyone else for your mistakes. Do take responsibility for every aspect of your life. Simply live by your principles, morals, and ethics; usually everything else will fall into place and you'll never have any regrets.

4. Have a positive attitude.

Thinking positively can have the most incredible effect on your health, wealth, and happiness. Keep an optimistic outlook on life. Thinking that there is a lesson in everything that happens can inspire you to greater things than ever before. Winners have positive attitudes. As Norman Vincent Peale said, "If you think you can, you're right!"

5. Continuously learn.

Every successful person throughout history was probably a lifelong learner. Be a sponge: continue to learn from all aspects of life—spiritually, physically, emotionally, intellectually, and professionally. You can learn something from formal and informal means. Yes, books, classes, seminars, etc., can be very useful in maintaining and gaining in your career and home life, but there is also much to be learned from everyday experiences, interactions with people, and spiritual growth. Try to "learn something new every day."

6. Work hard.

Work hard at something you enjoy while leveraging your talents. There's nothing worse than making a career of something you dislike. Your disdain will show through in your work and will taint your business, personal, and spiritual life. Rather, find something that you truly enjoy for your career. There are online personality tests that will help you discover your strengths and weaknesses, your capabilities, and your talents. Just be sure to take a couple of these tests if you have no idea what you want to do in life! If you love your job, it will show through, as well. Your work will be better, more thorough, and probably more creative. Learn the difference between having a job and having a career. It takes guts, hard work, and persistence to achieve your goals. "Success is a journey, not a destination," as Arthur Robert Ashe, Jr. said.

7. Have faith.

Believe in yourself, your idea of God, and your country. Faith gives you the courage of conviction and the ability to stand alone when taking the big risks in life (and what other kinds are there?). Having faith means you can persevere in spite of great odds until your goal is achieved. Having faith means that you can always find another way to solve a problem. "Where there's a will, there's a way!"

8. Develop your character.

Character is something that is forged over a lifetime: it is a journey of "trials and tribulations" as we learn lessons from life experiences—easy lessons and hard lessons. Character can be defined as responsibility, discipline, integrity, honesty, ethics, trustworthiness, humility, courtesy, and morals, among other things. All of these require choices—the right choices. In the beginning we had our parents. As with most of us, our parents had a huge impact on our early lives, and mine were no different. Although our family was impacted by divorce, my mom was always there for my siblings and me in several important ways. She was an early champion of the Junior Miss motto of "be your best self" in that she never let us settle for using less than 100% of our God-given talents. We learned that it wasn't important to be the smartest person in class, but it was crucial to try our hardest to succeed and to learn from our mistakes. We learned the value of integrity, honesty, and courtesy in dealing with both family and friends—a result of Mom's high expectations and a little old-fashioned discipline, too rarely seen these days. To this day, I can't even tell a white lie, because she'd look me in the eye and know if I were telling the truth or not. Mom also educated us by example. She treated everyone with dignity and worth, whether it were an Army General or a busboy, and I strive to embody this great quality of hers. As I grew up, life choices became harder: sex before marriage, résumé puffery, dating someone at work (or not), divorce, faking time cards or expense reports, or even padding the business numbers. (Hint: the answer for all of these is "don't!") Your faith, foundation, and personal growth will allow you to take on these challenges and lead you to make the best choice. But remember, there's no right way to do the wrong thing. So, rise to each occasion with character, humor, and love. "Talk the talk and walk the walk." Oh, and by the way, don't do anything that wouldn't make your mother proud!

9. Innovate.

Everyone has the potential to "think big," whether you're a child prodigy or more like the rest of us. Creativity and innovation are the keys to moving civilization forward, and your ideas can make the difference. IBM's slogan of "innovation that matters" can be a mantra—IBM'ers respect "wild ducks." The wild duck may fly against the grain (or the flock), but sometimes that wild duck finds the better air for the entire flock. Look for new ways to do things and to do them better. It's fun, too. "Think outside of the box."

10. Marry the right person.

There really is a Prince Charming for each of us. Don't listen to the media or your friends when they say there's no such thing, that it's okay to settle for second best. Wrong, wrong, wrong! The person you choose to marry is THE decision that will affect 90% of your success or lead to 100% of your misery. There are several areas to consider in knowing whether your beau is the right one for you:

Do you have common goals, interests, and values? Even though it may be exciting to date someone very different from yourself, it is difficult to base a lifetime on differences rather than commonalities.

Do you trust him? Is he trustworthy? Being able to trust your partner allows you to give 110% to your relationship. It allows you to grow together as one. Suspicion and jealousy can quickly destroy relationships, and you don't want to discover this *after* you're married.

Do you have mutual respect? Long-term relationships require thinking about the other person more than yourself. Think about how you are when you are together: are you arguing or competing against each other? Are you dressing down your partner or suffering physical or emotional abuse? Having civil discussions about disagreements is healthy; perpetual arguing is not.

Ask yourself: How do you feel when you are with him? Respected, important, loved, cared for? Or used, unworthy, ashamed, scared?

What do other people in your life think about him? Family and friends can often be more objective than you can, especially when you're in love. Just be sure to ask them for their honest opinions and don't be satisfied with platitudes.

Don't get married merely because your friends are. Take your time. Be picky. Like the song says, "My mama told me, you'd better shop around." There is rarely a good reason to marry too quickly. I have to say that my personal dating experiences were pretty dismal in my teens and twenties, so who am I to give advice? My sister got it right. "Marry your best friend," she said. (And she did—she's been married 25 years!) I always thought that was the dumbest thing I ever heard, and it came from my younger sister, yet. But her advice was true. In my late thirties, I met the man I'd marry and didn't even realize it. We were good friends for three years before we started dating—and in those three years, we enjoyed each other's company, got to know each other's idiosyncrasies and, well, things just clicked one day. We fell in love, we respected each other, we enjoyed similar tastes and hobbies, and we even worked in related professions. He's sensitive, intelligent, handsome, and funny—he is truly the right man for me, and I've never been happier. Moral of the story: wait long enough and you will find your soul mate. Set your sights high, and don't settle for second best in love, business, or life! In the words of James M. Barrie, "If you have love, you don't need to have anything else; and if you don't have love, it doesn't matter much what else you have."

In conclusion . . .

The things I am most proud of are the character my upbringing built and my education—they are the foundation for all my achievements and have enabled me to rise to the challenges of life and enjoy it to the fullest. Over the years, I've earned a bachelor's degree in Computer Science from Penn State, a master's degree from the University of Southern California, and a Ph.D. from George Washington University. I was proud to serve my country as a Captain in the U.S. Marine Corps, and I've had the privilege of working at IBM for the last 29 years with some of the most talented and smart people in the industry. I have run a marathon, lived all over the United States, traveled to Europe, Asia, and Latin America, completed many home improvement projects, learned the art of dressage, and studied Tae Kwon Do. Nowadays, I enjoy open-road racing, crossword puzzles and Sudoku, volunteering for Junior Miss projects, playing the piano, skiing, biking, and hiking the trails in my home of Lake Tahoe (I really need to work on my cooking, though). But the best part of success is sharing it! I've been very happily married to my soul mate, Dave, for over 13 years.

So I must finish now with two of my favorite corny, but wise, sayings: "Success is not the key to happiness. Happiness is the key to success. If you love what you are doing, you will be successful" (Albert Schweitzer). And finally, "Just do it!" (Nike).

Dr. Linda Rutledge Delbridge represented Kansas when she was chosen to be America's Junior Miss in 1973. She used her scholarship money throughout her educational endeavors. Linda graduated magna cum laude from Pennsylvania State University with a B.S. in Computer Science and a minor in Electrical Engineering.

Upon completion of Officer Candidate School, she was commissioned as a Second Lieutenant in the United States Marine Corps. She served for four years with duty stations in Quantico, VA and Camp Pendleton, CA, where she managed the West Coast Teleprocessing Network. During this time, she obtained her M.S. in Systems Management from the University of Southern California.

In 1980, Linda was hired by IBM Corporation's Federal Systems Division in Washington, DC, as Technical Assistant to the Director of Advanced Programs. Over the last 28+ years with IBM, she has held multiple management and staff positions. In 1985, she was named an Outstanding Young Woman of America.

With the help of IBM's Graduate Work Study Program, she completed her doctorate in Computer Science, with minors in Engineering Administration and Artificial Intelligence through George Washington University in 1987. Linda is currently a Business Development Executive and Certi-fied Project Manager at the executive level with IBM's End User Service, Service Product Line, part of Global Technology Solutions.

On February 14, 1996, Linda and David Delbridge were married at Lake Tahoe, NV, where they currently reside with their two Alaskan Malamutes.

Linda has served as a panel evaluator for numerous state and local programs and five times at the national America's Junior Miss program.

Giving Back

21

The Fragrance of Success

Lenne Jo Hallgren Best

The air was crisp and my roses were budding! It even looked as if, by late in the afternoon, one would blossom. Yes, spring was in the air. I loved springtime. The day was a bright and beautiful Sunday morning. My children were freshly scrubbed and in the backseat with their seatbelts fastened, which wasn't always an easy task—but we had accomplished it, and we were off to church! The evidence of new life was all around, ready to take root and burst forth. How I loved the beauty of spring and the promise of all that is new and fresh. For me it is food for the soul. Just give me a shovel, a little dirt, and something to plant. Toss in some water and then sit back and watch something magnificent happen—the miracle of life.

After delivering my kids to their Sunday school classes, I carefully endeavored to get seated. Balancing coffee in one hand and Bible in the other, I was just in the knick of time. I was never good at being early. But I am always good at cutting it really close. I took a deep breath and tried to focus. The hymns were especially moving today. We had had a good thunder and lightning show the night before, so the air was clean. I took another deep breath and thought how wonderful this morning was!

Pastor Roper was known for his sermons throughout the Northwest. He was direct, creative, and captivating. I looked forward to what he would have to say today. It was *spring* for goodness sake. In a few weeks it would be time to cut my roses with their vibrant colors and place them in a vase on my dining room table for all to see and enjoy. Did I tell you how much I love my roses? Well, I do! Then the pastor spoke. I couldn't believe what I was hearing. All hope seemed to be dashed in a moment. "Life is hard and then you die." What? Did I hear him correctly? Yep, he said, "Life is hard and then you die."

Ten years after that vibrant spring morning, I was seated at my dining room table. No roses. It had been an extremely long winter. It was April and still no glimpse of spring. How disheartening. Yet I knew that the promise of changing seasons was almost here. The past week had been a difficult one. I had just returned from my hometown of Clarkston, Washington, where I had buried my mom, who had died in a tragic car accident. I had lost my best friend, my confidante, and my warrior. She was the one who loved me in spite of all circumstances. She was my encourager and the one who *always* saw the glass as half full. My three children were devastated. Grandma "B" never forgot a holiday, a birthday, a basketball game, or a baseball game. She was either there in person or there in spirit. We will have to settle for the latter now. We had talked every day—every single day. She was worth every penny of the phone bill.

After her death, I realized she had helped me define success. It is *not* about what we *get*; it is about what we *give* without expecting *anything* in return. It is about letting go, and letting God direct the path of one's life. He says that even our hairs are numbered. C'mon, our hairs? So He says! Yep, life is hard and then you die. Yet, He loves us so. I know it to be true. Just because life is hard, it doesn't mean that it can't be fun, exhilarating, and at times moving. Above all else, you can use your life to support, encourage, and love others to a higher calling. That is what my mom did unlike anyone I have ever known. She could move in, unnoticed, and then *bam*, she had you. Her love was a perfect example of unconditional, I don't care what you think, kind of love. She understood pain and hurting. She met you right where you were—good, bad, or indifferent. It's hard to believe she was an only child. Don't some people consider them spoiled from birth?

Memories of my mom transport me back thirty years. I had just won the Clarkston Junior Miss title. It was the fall of 1975. As a little girl, my mom had taken me to watch the program. I loved the sparkling crown and the banner. Oh, yes, and I loved the roses, as well as being crowned as something good and worthwhile. I had not only won the title and valuable scholarship money, but I also had the support of those who were competing with me. I was given the Spirit of Junior Miss award that was voted on by my fellow contenders. While the Junior Miss program is not a beauty pageant, for one night on stage in formal attire, it was every little girl's dream come true. And for this little girl, it was on to the state competition.

My mom's advice was always, "Just be yourself and have fun! Do your best. Whatever happens, happens. The experience will change your life. Enjoy it and appreciate all the new people that you are about to meet. This is a once-in-a-lifetime experience!" And so I heeded her advice. I was myself and I had fun. Before I knew it, it *had* changed my life—forever! I had won the state program and was on my way to the national competition. My hometown was behind me. I had the prayerful support of my friends. It was an amazing time of responsibility and excitement. I was afraid, and then I remembered what my mom had said: "Just be yourself. Do your best." And, oh, I did.

I'll never forget Nationals and Michael Landon. Need I say more? He was the master of ceremonies for the CBS Primetime program. There he was, Mr. Little-House-on-the-Prairie himself, and I was in the top seven finalists! He cleared his voice and said, "Now meet America's Junior Miss for 1976 . . . (the pause seemed almost life threatening) Lenne Jo Hallgren—of Clarkston, Washington!" A crown, two dozen roses, a banner, and a year packed full of wondrous opportunities were given to me. I think that's when I fell in love with roses. They were so fragrant, so fresh, and so beautiful. The whole moment was timeless. As I walked down the runway, I caught my mother's eyes. Tears. More excitement. With a smile and a wave, I was forever changed.

What do we do when life has been so good and now we find it so hard? When someone we love dies, what do we write about? Do we see the glass as half empty—or half full? Do we choose to make a difference in our lives and in the lives of others? When things are difficult, do we see the bright side of a cloudy day? Success to me is holding onto all that is good and somehow passing it on to all those around us, either by a smile, by a comforting word, or by slowly pouring goodness into the soul of another—like my mother did.

I am so grateful for the opportunity to have been America's Junior Miss. I am even more thankful to have been the daughter of a mother who chose to make sure that I understood that sacrifice, dignity, and self-worth are above selfishness and "fifteen minutes of fame." My mother was able to comprehend the value of a person and the enduring worth of a soul. She knew that she would blossom and ultimately fade, and that the withered petals would still be fragrant enough to impart wonderful memories of a life lived to its full potential.

That is why I love roses, even those that have seen better days. Though dried and withered, they still impart a beauty having made the most of what they were while they had the opportunity. Amazingly, their fragrance lingers, underscoring that our success is intertwined with those around us. How incredibly wonderful is life on this side of heaven's doors—and how incredibly hard. Be encouraged to know that the *fragrance* of life truly comes once we pass to the other side. What aroma of encouragement will you leave behind? Success will be what you make of it to build up those around you. My mother lived it, and I have been its recipient.

She will be the first to greet me once I am there on the other side—with roses. You wanna bet?

While serving as America's Junior Miss of 1976, Lenne Jo Hallgren Best appeared on The Tonight Show, Good Morning America, To Tell the Truth, *and* The Stars and Stripes Show. *On July 4th that same year, she celebrated our nation's 200th birthday with President Ford, Charlton*

Heston, Mean Joe Green, and Marion Anderson and represented the youth of our country by delivering a speech at Independence Hall just prior to the President addressing our nation on this momentous occasion.

As the last Breck Girl, Lenne Jo was on the cover of Coed Magazine *and appeared in* Teen, Seventeen, People, *and* Reader's Digest. *She graduated from Whitworth College with a degree in Speech Communications and a minor in English.*

Lenne Jo has worked in radio, television, public relations, and most recently, custom jewelry design. She has guest authored several books. While attending the All-American Rose Selection in New York City, Lenne Jo was presented with over twelve dozen roses from Princess Grace of Monico. No wonder she fell in love with roses!

22

Serving Your Country

Andrea Plummer, M.D.

I have always been a patriot. I'm not sure when I first recognized this fact, but perhaps it was when I heard other girls singing "Mary Had a Little Lamb" while I chanted the lyrics of the "Air Force Fight Song": "Off we go into the wild blue yonder!" I remember the day my dad taught me those words, and so began my love for America and my respect for the U.S. military. Growing up, I didn't know that I would ultimately commit myself to a career serving as an Air Force physician. What I did realize is how fortunate we are to live in a country that values freedom and humanity, and I wanted to find a unique way to preserve those values.

When people hear that someone "serves her country," they often assume that the individual is a member of the U.S. military. While wearing a uniform and standing on the front lines of battle is the ultimate demonstration of patriotism, there is another way to serve our country—through day-to-day volunteerism. Through my experiences in high school, college, and beyond, I have learned that to be an effective volunteer, you must follow a few simple steps: (1) identify a need; (2) define your unique skills; (3) enjoy the fulfillment of putting your skills into action; and (4) recognize that patriotism is a lifelong commitment.

Identify a Need

Look around your community. Are there children without healthcare? Are there people without homes? Are there teens without mentors? Every community has needs, though they may be quite different from one to the next. When identifying a specific need, look for something that inspires you and that motivates you to act. Commitment to a cause requires a passion for making a difference. Don't do something because your parents or friends think it's important. Look around you and into your heart, and search for a need that you are desperate to fulfill. When I was a college student, I learned about an organization that matches students with elderly people in nursing homes. The "Adopt-a-Grandparent" program allowed me to visit one lady in particular whose family members were either deceased or living far away. She never had visitors, so my weekly visits provided her with a chance to talk, ask questions, and share her amazing life experiences with me. She sang to me (since at one time she was very active in her church choir), and I performed ballet for her and her fellow residents. Words can't express the mutual joy of that relationship. She was approaching the end of her life, and I could provide her with the love and respect that she deserved. Look around you. Talk to members of your community. Find a need that excites you. You may just have the skills to fill it.

Define Your Unique Skills

We've all been blessed with unique talents and traits. Are you really good at talking to people? Are you an active listener? How are you at fundraising? Perhaps you are great at number crunching, or you are talented in the arts. The best volunteers align their skills with the needs of the community. If you are shy, why try to approach strangers to raise money when you might be better at using your hands to actually build homes for people? I learned fairly early on that I am NOT shy. Just ask my parents. Approaching strangers is something that comes naturally for me. Therefore, I often chose experiences where I could reach out to new people, like tutoring younger students while in high school, visiting an elderly woman during college, and educating families with the National Multiple Sclerosis Society during medical school. It's also important to draw from your own individual life experiences. My personal experience supporting my mother, who has multiple sclerosis, gave me the knowledge and understanding to reach out to other families battling the disease. For that reason, I committed a year of my life after college to providing patient and family education through the National MS Society. So lean on what you know, what you've experienced, and what you feel that you can uniquely offer. By doing that, you'll enjoy the process of volunteering while offering better service to your community.

Enjoy Putting Your Skills into Action

Remember when I mentioned how much I liked visiting my "adopted grandmother" while in college? Volunteerism is not only about fulfilling a need in a community. It can be fun and rewarding! A friend of mine who committed his time to Habitat for Humanity once stated that the best moment for him in each project was seeing that last nail get hammered into the house. He loved the sight of a brand new home that he had helped to build. We've all been blessed with talents. Our challenge in life is to find the best way to utilize those abilities. Many people spend half their lives trying to find the best possible job, a career that matches their skills and talents with the needs of the workplace. Why is this? Because we all desire the satisfaction of feeling that there is purpose in our lives, a reason that we have been made the way we are. Volunteerism offers us an opportunity to have purpose in our community and give back to the people around us. Enjoy the experience!

Recognize That Patriotism Is a Lifelong Commitment

Someone once asked me how I defined patriotism. I responded that the very meaning of the word is "a love for one's country." That begins on the most basic level by loving the community around you and by finding small ways to serve the people in it. We've discussed the important steps in being an effective volunteer. What I'd like to leave you with is a reminder that volunteering should be a lifelong devotion.

When I entered medical school, I continued to look for ways to use my skills in order to serve my community. The memory of the "Air Force Fight Song" often came into my head, along with memories of growing up on Air Force bases as my dad pursued a career as a pilot. I recognized my desire to serve in the military but wondered if my skills aligned with the career of a pilot or combat officer. I investigated the various opportunities in the military and discovered that there is a great need for physicians of all specialties. Specifically, pediatricians are always in great demand because the children of our men and women in uniform require frequent medical care as they grow and develop. I saw a future where I could utilize my personality traits and medical knowledge to serve a unique group of patients. The next thing I knew, I was being sworn in as a Second Lieutenant by my father at the downtown recruiting station in New York City. Since then, I have not looked back. I am proud of the work I do every day; and though it has its challenges and its setbacks, I am thankful for the opportunity to show how much I love my amazing country. So wave your flags on the 4th of July! Hang yellow ribbons to support our troops! But more importantly, throughout the many stages of your life, find a need in the community around you, and strive to use your gifts to fulfill it. Be a true patriot. Our country depends on it.

> Patriotism . . . is not short, frenzied outbursts of emotion, but the tranquil and steady dedication of a lifetime.
>
> —*Adlai Stevenson*

Andrea Plummer, M.D., is a pediatrician and Captain in the Air Force. She served as America's Junior Miss in 1996. Andrea received a Bachelor of Arts from the University of Virginia in 2000. She was Miss New York 2001 and placed fourth runner-up at the Miss America Pageant. Andrea graduated with an M.D. from Albany Medical College in 2006 and began her three-year residency in San Diego, CA as an active duty Air Force pediatrician. She is enjoying her first official assignment at Nellis Air Force Base, NV, where she provides medical care to the children of active duty service members.

23

From Selling Cookies to Saving the World

Nina Vasan

When I think about my personal definition of success, one clear idea comes to mind—bettering our world. My role models are people who have fought for equality, reduced poverty, protected the environment, and saved lives. My own efforts to better our world range from my childhood days of dressing up as a daffodil and selling flowers in my local mall for the American Cancer Society's "Daffodil Days" fundraiser to my current project, creating the *Saving the World* series of books on leadership and social change. One of the forces that helped to shape my understanding of the importance of working to better our world most, that helped me to discover my definition of success, is the Girl Scouts.

My Girl Scouting experience began 18 years ago in Vienna, West Virginia, in first grade, when I ran from school to my mom's car, and she presented me with a brown sash and a golden trefoil pin that I would wear at my first Brownie meeting. Twelve years later, I found myself in Washington, DC, receiving the Girl Scouts Young Woman of Distinction award from Justice Sandra Day O'Connor; presenting the Woman of Distinction award to Girl Scout and Senator Elizabeth Dole; and meeting extraordinary women and men who championed the values of scouting.

In the twelve years that I spent in Brownies, Juniors, and Cadettes, Girl Scouts has given me many things. For starters, it gave me a group of girls to grow up with; our shared memories include everything from dolls, cute boys, and high heels, to cleaning up the Ohio River and educating classmates on domestic policy aimed at improving social welfare. Girl Scouts gave me a love for color coding, which began with the cookie order forms, color coded by cookie: Do-Si-Do orange, Samoa purple, Trefoil gold, etc. This love for color coding has continued—as my Google calendar will reveal, my daily schedule is similarly color coded with Harvard Medical School red, Obama Presidential Campaign blue, and Saving the World Book Series green. Girl Scouts gave me an appreciation for the culinary genius of combining chocolate with mint in the form of a perfectly rounded thin mint cookie. And Girl Scouts taught me that Hollywood movies are not reality; and that even though Troop Beverly Hills got to stay in a five-star hotel instead of camping outside, I did not have the same option, even if I did forget my insect repellant.

But when it comes to succeeding in the real world, there are three more significant things that Girl Scouts gave me, and these three are articulated in the closing lines of the Girl Scout Law: *I will do my best, to make the world a better place, and be a sister to every Girl Scout.*

So I'd like to talk to you about three things: (1) doing your best, (2) making the world a better place, and (3) being a sister to every Girl Scout.

Do Your Best

Consider the many multicolored badges that fill the vests and sashes of Girl Scouts. The "Try-It" badge, or project interest award, gives the girl a concrete goal to work towards. Each girl's path to earning a badge is unique, and she is given the option to choose which requirements she will fulfill. This choice (talk to a politician, educate your classmates, or write a letter to the editor) shows girls the importance of setting a goal and doing your best, your own personal best. It shows that we can be equally successful earning the same badge, by taking our own unique paths. Further, as one girl may work towards "Emergency Preparedness" while another toward "Eco Action," we get to create our own definitions of success. This taught me how to respect myself and my own best, and just as importantly, how to admire and appreciate the best in others.

In elementary school I was glued to the TV, following strong young women who showed their best to me, to you, and to the world. As role models like Michelle Kwan and Dominique Dawes were twirling and tumbling their way to World and Olympic gold on the ice rink and balance beam, unknown West Virginian gymnast Nina Vasan was practicing how to achieve her own perfect landing—jumping down four or five stairs of the basement staircase (six stairs on an especially brave day), making sure to land with both feet together, pausing, smiling, and then throwing her hands in the air to acknowledge the judges and fans (or in my case one fan, my brother Neil who would kindly remind me that the extent of my gymnastics ability—a somersault—was not a part of any gold-medal routine). Olympic gold was not in my future, but through Girl Scouts I was able to "go for the gold" as well, the Gold Award. I found that where I could excel was through service to the community and leadership. Through Girl Scouts I was able to appreciate and admire the best of incredible athletes like Kwan and Dawes, take pride in my own talents and contributions, and never have regret as long as I did my best.

Make the World a Better Place

The second thing Girl Scouts taught me was the importance of trying to make the world a better place. The heart of my Girl Scouting experience was in building a community and giving back to that community, that is valuing and acting on social responsibility. These are values that were instilled in me by my family—my dad, the head of a charitable foundation; my mom, a board member of the Parkersburg Community Foundation and a coleader of my Brownie troop; and my brother, an Eagle Scout. And these values were shared by my community in West Virginia. Girl Scouts reinforced my family's and community's values.

In trying to make the world a better place, my own experiences have ranged from serving as the National President of American Cancer Society Teens, the nationwide network of student volunteers for our country's largest voluntary health organization, to presenting my scientific research during the Nobel Prize Festivities, to creating The Mountaineer Fund, a 501(c)3 organization that invests raised capital and provides management consulting to entities aimed at using social entrepreneurship to improve equality, health, education, environment, and economy in my native West Virginia. We all have a responsibility to improve the world, starting with our communities. And through Girl Scouts I have seen that "making the world a better place" is not just some naïve or idealistic notion; it is a real, tangible thing that we all can and must do.

Be a Sister to Every Girl Scout

Finally, we come to the idea of being a sister to every Girl Scout. When I think about my future, I focus on this idea: the sisterhood, the need to support women, all women, from school girls here in America to mothers in Sudan and Iraq.

When I became a Girl Scout, there were only two women serving in the 100-member United States Senate and only one female CEO of a Fortune 500 company. Fast forward 18 years. Today we are living at a monumental moment in time when American women have surpassed men in college enrollment, and we have women heads of state on every continent as well as a strong and brilliant woman who received 18 million votes for President of our United States. Women have made great progress, but we aren't done yet. There exist significant inequalities in our financial, political, and professional freedoms. And much of this is the result of deeply embedded gender discrimination.

What can we do about it? Well, gender is a social construct, an idea created by society. And since society, all of "us," created gender, we also have the ability to *change* gender. So I would like to challenge you, girls and boys alike, to try to change gender in favor of more equality and freedom for women—women who, be they West Virginia

Mountaineers or citizens of countries far away, are our sisters, a part of us, and for whom we need to honor by fighting for true equality.

So what is success? Success is doing your best, making the world a better place, and being a sister to every girl. Success is doing your part and contributing to saving the world.

An American Cancer Society volunteer since kindergarten, Nina Vasan, 24, served as the National President of American Cancer Society Teens, creating a nationwide network of student leaders in community organizing, fundraising, public health education, and political advocacy. As CEO of The Mountaineer Fund, a new organization that invests raised capital in social entrepreneurs, Nina successfully initiated and directed the effort to keep the Master Tobacco Settlement funds reserved for disease treatment, prevention, and health education in her home state of West Virginia. Nina is the creator and coauthor of the upcoming Saving the World *series of books on leadership and social change. A member of Barack Obama's Health Policy Advisory Committee, she was cochair of Battleground State Outreach for the 2008 Presidential Campaign.*

Nina's scientific involvement includes presenting her research at the Nobel Prize Festivities and helping to direct policy and publication of the New England Journal of Medicine. *A former Research Fellow at the Angiogenesis Foundation, she has coauthored over a dozen research papers and abstracts and serves on the National Advisory Board for Cogito.org, a community for exceptionally talented young scientists and mathematicians. Nina worked in Geneva for Dr. Margaret Chan, Director-General of the World Health Organization, where she developed a plan for UN Secretary General Ban Ki-Moon on strategically advancing progress towards the Millennium Development Goals.*

An Olympic torchbearer and West Virginia's Junior Miss, Nina has been named as one of our country's top young leaders by the Girl Scouts, Glamour, CosmoGirl, Time Inc., *and* USA Today; *was inducted into the Hall of Fame for Caring Americans; and is the subject of five books and documentaries. She studied Government at Harvard College and is a second-year MD/MBA student at Harvard Medical School and Harvard*

Business School. Nina's favorite things include NPR, nutella, afternoon naps, online bargain hunting, Mad Men, *and* Friday Night Lights.

24

Give Me Some Lovin'

Linde Caitlin Groover

Throughout the course of your day, I can assure you that you are likely to come in contact with one of the following things: peers or parents who are too critical, jeans that are too tight, or the occasional fall-down-the-stairs-in-front-of-everyone moment, which is always *way* too embarrassing to play off. Let's face it: life is clumsy.

Yet in a world of such clumsiness, we are often brought up to measure success by our ability to avoid the mishaps of our lives. I am here to tell you that it's time to stop fixing yourself. Stop for a moment and learn to love.

This advice might seem a bit different from what you hear from parents, teachers, or peers, and it is certainly not easy to comprehend. If you're anything like me, the competitive spirit inside you is saying something like this: *No WAY is success about love! Success is winning! It's being the best! It's overcoming, overcompensating, overpowering!* I was truly convinced that this voice inside of my head was right. This mentality is what brought me to several years of feeling lost, inadequate, and unhopeful. Especially in my teenage years, I was never skinny enough, never a fast enough swimmer, never a good enough writer, never a good enough student. I had developed a skewed perception of what it meant to be successful until a turning point in my life: a car accident that caused my older sister and best friend, Brittany, to experience an untimely death. In her passing, Brittany's friends and family did not always remember how many medals she won in soccer, or that she had decent grades, or that she had the most fashionable wardrobe of all her friends. What they remembered was when she said hello to strangers in the hallway at school, when she helped a friend after her boyfriend dumped her, and when she listened to an elderly member for hours at church—even if she had loads of homework to squeeze in that Sunday afternoon.

Needless to say, this experience still constantly forces me to reevaluate what is truly important in my life. What will people remember about me? Perhaps some will remember that I was Class President, a Junior Miss, a straight "A" student, an accomplished pianist, and a record holder for swimming and soccer. But more will remember what actually mattered—*who* I helped, *what* I gave, and *how much* I loved. As I near the end of my first year at the University of Virginia, I have developed the following mentality: making lasting friends outweighs making perfect grades; being my Best Self outweighs being *the* best; loving my body outweighs perfecting it; and as a swim coach and tutor, fun and improvement outweigh winning. Although I miss my sister dearly, I have come out on a brighter side from her death, and I am here to urge you to redefine success as a measure of love in your life, not of accolades. In the end, people will remember what and who you loved, not what you did.

Seems like a bit too much to love yourself and everyone (and everything) around you, even on the worst of days? I agree. I struggle with it myself. But you have all of the strength and love that you will ever need inside you at this moment. Never sell yourself short of your value as a loving human being, and never feel insignificant if you fail to conquer the world. Because, while the world may not remember your name, someone will. And in order to leave a positive example behind, you must leave behind the barriers in your life. Leave behind fear of failure, selfishness, and doubt—for the point of absolute certainty never arrives. Above all else, leave behind your differences to make room for love. Love more than you think you should, for your love is worth leaving behind for those who mean the world to you. If we can build a future rich in love for those following us, the love we leave behind will live in the lives of our children, and that's something worth leaving for the world.

How do you construct a life of love? Your construction will be as unique as you are. While there is no set formula for creating a life of love, I can certainly give you a starting point: The first step in learning to love daily and putting aside definitions of success is to make what I call a "grateful list." I'm sure you're a champ when it comes to making "to-do" lists—they are essential in goal setting and goal achieving—but taking just five minutes before you start your day to write a list of what you are grateful for focuses your mind on what you should love in life and what you have completed, rather than what you are missing or what you need to do. Are you grateful for friends? A good night's sleep? Finishing that book report? Having cute ankles or a good hair day or having hair at all? Think on these things each morning, and you will start to see your mind focus more upon the loves of your life, rather than the unfinished tasks or imperfections.

So forget the money; forget the skinniest skinny you could possibly achieve; forget grace or fame or perfection. At the end of the day, what truly matters is that you give yourself and others love—and lots of it! A successful young lady is not the one who has life figured out: she does not always have the perfect friends, the perfect boyfriend, the perfect grades, or the perfect skin; she is the one who has imperfect friends but loves them anyway, who doesn't need a man to measure her worth, who loves learning more than grades, and who has flawed skin but still smiles at herself in the mirror. A successful young lady forgets about "figuring life out" and remembers each day that, in life, we must love along the way. I have found that once one begins this way of life, the rest of life's pleasures will fall (surprisingly, gracefully) into place.

Linde Groover is a fourth-year Echols Scholar at the University of Virginia and is currently pursuing a degree in Biomedical Ethics and Cross Cultural Healing. She is a member of the National Society of Collegiate Scholars, the Phi Eta Sigma *Honor Fraternity, and the Golden Key*

International Honour Society. As a Lawn Resident at the University of Virginia, Linde holds the highest undergraduate honor at UVa.

Linde participates in Camp Kesem at the University of Virginia, a student-run camp that serves children of cancer patients. A former cochair and National Student Advisory Board Representative for Camp Kesem, she continues to serve the organization as a volunteer counselor and fundraiser. Linde is a member of Pi Beta Phi *at UVa and currently serves on UVa's Inter-Sorority Council's executive board, promoting the positive aspects of Greek Life to both the student body and the local community. She is also a volunteer soccer coach and mentors teens and college students.*

A former resident of Forest, Virginia, Linde has a younger sister, Carly, and two loving parents, Tim and Beth Groover. She enjoys traveling, writing, scrapbooking, Seal Team Physical Training, and yoga. Her life goal is to motivate children to reach their full potential, and she is on a perpetual search for innovative ways to realize that goal.

25

Success Has a Sound

Lea Mack Compton

Her hospital bed was pushed off to the side of the dingy, one-room apartment with the window next to her head open to allow in the gentle, spring breeze. Her 30-year-old body, filled with cancer, tied her fragile spirit to this world with chords about to give way. The respirator, assisting her breathing, supported the tension between her divorced parents with a steady rhythm, setting the scene for my music therapy.

Her pain was everywhere that day in spite of the morphine. She asked if we could visit the ocean again, as we had in our last session, and I began to play my guitar. My melody was simple; her breath set the pace. We staggered into our journey together, uncertain at first, and finally settling into sync with each other. I could feel the sounds lifting us from the dark room, carrying us to a better place.

The gentle music began to paint pictures in my mind of the rolling surf, cool breeze, and warm sun of the place she called home. I began to sing about the pictures, a few words at a time, cautious not to disrupt the deeper breathing I could now see in her delicate frame. She relaxed more, imagining the sun on her face and surf on her feet. Her breathing slowed, and she began to drift—at one with the music.

Her mother and father noticed the change and came to the bed. Careful to keep their distance from each other, the grieving mother stood at the foot and the father stood at the side, both touching their child, trying to connect in the final moments. I asked if there were any thoughts they wanted to share with their daughter, and her mother tearfully whispered, "I love you." Her words inspired musical lyrics, "You are loved." Her mother joined me in singing them, her voice now pure and strong.

Her father added words like, "You are so strong," and "I am proud of you." I sang them as I had the others, and a connection occurred. Her mother, caught up in the moment, sang her father's words with as much strength and conviction as she had her own. For a few precious moments, they were a family on a journey together.

The music therapy had done its work for my patient several minutes ago; this moment belonged to her parents. This was a moment of healing and peace; anger, resentment, and strife were gone. Healing has a sound, and this day it included the words of a father, the voice of a mother, the breath of a child, and the guitar of a music therapist.

Success for me, as a music therapist, is measured in terms of sound. I understand this more today than ever; but still, I knew from a young age my musical gifts could make a difference. Before I even finished my sophomore English research paper on music therapy, I was hooked; music therapy was for me. I knew I would find success in making a difference with the gifts that I possessed, but convincing those around me was a different story. You see, to achieve success, you must be willing to use your gifts to make the kind of impact that means the most to you even when others don't understand.

Discovering Your Gifts

Musical talents are public and easy to recognize. School plays, church musicals, and even programs like Junior Miss were good venues for me to demonstrate my gifts. Not all gifts are public, however. For example, organization, motivation, compassion, sensitivity, academics, and many other gifts are at their best with few people watching. Behind the scenes does not mean unimportant, so using your gifts means you have to recognize them even if nobody else does.

Many do not have the first clue what their gifts are. If you figure yours out, you are way ahead of most of the people around you. However, it can be a challenge to figure them out. Our weaknesses, on the other hand, seem to stand out like a cell phone ringing in the middle of a romantic scene at the movies. They get all our attention, and we spend huge amounts of time and energy trying to cover them up so no one else notices. All this time spent worrying about weaknesses takes our attention off of our strengths, making our gifts difficult to recognize. There are three types of weaknesses: acceptable, fixable, and disastrous. Knowing what yours are can keep them from blocking your discovery of your true gifts.

Disastrous weaknesses are the ones that deeply affect your life. No, your nose is not one of these. These are weaknesses that make it impossible for you to function, such as alcoholism, drug addiction, willingness to tolerate abuse, and others requiring serious help to correct. If you have any of these, you need to get help now, before you finish this chapter, or you will never be able to use your wonderful, unique gifts.

Fixable weaknesses are often strengths waiting to be discovered. Some things about our personalities can get us into trouble; but with some effort, we can overcome them. Often the attention we give them makes them useful to us later on. Talking is one of my fixable weaknesses. Do you remember the student who had to sit at a desk facing the wall, away from the rest of the class? I was that kid until seventh grade. That's right, even my sixth grade English teacher separated me because I could not keep my mouth shut.

I love to talk, and I've always had something to say. Unfortunately, I said it to whomever I wanted whenever it suited me. I had no respect for the proper time and place for my conversations. I had to learn when to keep my mouth shut, and eventually I did. Now I get paid to talk. I still have to hold my tongue when the timing is not right, but I do get many opportunities to talk until I'm blue in the face, and people seem to love it. I have worked so hard at fixing this weakness that now it has become a gift.

Acceptable weaknesses are ones you have tried to change and simply cannot: your nose, your ears, your athletic ability or lack of, your body, your family, and other similar characteristics. Welcome to the human race. We all have these things, and they make us lovable. Nobody likes perfect people because they make us feel bad about ourselves.

My most annoying, acceptable weakness is clumsiness. I am always spilling drinks, dropping food, and running into things. I try to pay attention on special occasions, but it only helps a little bit. Those who love me accept that dinner with me requires dishtowels, not napkins, and we get along just fine. Embrace the weaknesses that give you character and move on. They do not stand in the way of your gifts. Knowing our gifts is really easier than we make it once our weaknesses are out of the way. Answering these questions honestly will open your eyes to your gifts.

1.   What do you love to spend your time doing?
2.   What are you naturally good at?
3.   What do people compliment you on most often?

The answers to these questions point to your natural gifts, or natural strengths. Do not discount any of them because they seem unimportant or unpopular. You have a monopoly on what you have to offer, and monopolies are powerful. Nobody else has your set of strengths, making them unique and very important.

Using Your Gifts to Make an Impact

The fluorescent lighting droned, casting a greenish glow on the music therapy room. As an intern, I observed the scene from a shadowy corner. A phone could be heard ringing down the hall, and the occasional click of footsteps echoed off the cinderblock walls. Neat rows of braids rested on the man's head in contrast to the disorder and aggression of the swirling thoughts beneath them. He sat, with his guitar in position, ready to play; the hum of the amplifier signaled the time had come.

The heart of the music therapist beat so loudly, she was sure the schizophrenic patient could hear it. However, the screams in his mind drowned out all other sound, "Light a match. Burn this building down. She's weak. One hit with your guitar would finish her."

The music therapist gave the signal, and his guitar roared to life with strength and purpose. The beat was heavy, and the sound filled the room, overflowing into the halls of the locked psychiatric compound. Could he play loud enough to silence the voices within?

His mind began to focus, and he heard sound with structure and clarity for the first time in a week. The therapist saw him settle into the experience and encouraged him to keep playing. He was communicating. He made sense. He had not lost himself completely, as he had feared. His heart rose on the rich strains of music to a place where it could breathe again. His eyes were able to focus on the room for the first time, and he heard her ask him what direction their music should take that day. The decision was really his, for a change, and he made it.

They played for at least an hour, in a place of freedom and acceptance. The relief of order had taken the place of his raging, inner storm. Rescue has a sound, and this day it was a clear beat and a loud amplifier, supported by the drone of ordinary reality.

As I watched this scene from my corner, I knew this was the type of impact I wanted to make. I longed to be on the front lines, assisting someone's breakthrough. I wanted my hands in the action, and performing on a stage did not allow me the access I would need. I knew I could not save the world, but I felt confident I could help save a few. I desperately desired to be like the music therapist I had just seen in action.

Knowing your gifts and knowing your college major, or specific field of study, are two very different things. Once you've identified some of your gifts, you must decide what type of impact you want to make with them before you can pick a career. For example, I sing reasonably well, but I could not just major in singing. I had to choose between voice performance, musical theatre, music education, commercial music production, composition, music therapy, and the teaching of singing, to name a few.

I desire to make a person-to-person, let-me-help-you type of impact; I always have. My fondest memories of the musical productions from high school are not the onstage action but the backstage conversations with a friend fretting over a boy or struggling with parents. What about you? How do you like to make a difference? Are you drawn to one-to-one interaction? Do you prefer to impact a whole group—high profile or low profile? Do you seek immediate feedback? Do you like to contribute while no one is watching and then be recognized later? Are you content if no one ever knows your name as long as you can do your thing? Do you like working to avoid problems? How about fixing problems after they already exist?

Below, I've made a list of my music career options and the different impacts they would have allowed me to make, highlighting the types of interaction and impact I prefer most:

- High-profile group impact: performance or musical theatre.

- Low-profile group impact: music education, *music therapy.*

- No one watching, recognized later: composition, teaching of singing.

- Anonymous impact: commercial music production, composition.

- One-to-one interaction: *music therapy*, teaching of singing.

- Immediate feedback: performance or musical theatre, music education, *music therapy.*

- Working to avoid problems: performance or musical theatre, music education, commercial music production, composition, *music therapy*, teaching of singing.

- Fixing problems: commercial music production, composition, *music therapy*, teaching of singing.

Can you see why I chose music therapy? It is exactly how I like to operate. It allows me to make a contribution to the world in the most meaningful way to me. Most human beings want to be remembered for something; the ones we do remember did what they were good at in the way that was most gratifying for them. Before you select a career that sounds good, stop to consider the kind of life you want to live, how you like to interact with others, and the mark you're interested in leaving.

I have a young friend who is an undergraduate student with a major in biology and who has medical school aspirations. As she gets closer to applying to med school, she is considering many things: where she wants to live, her desire for a family, the boy she's dating, and her dream of being a doctor. She desperately wants to be a mother, and she would really like to stay in the South. She loves the idea of being a doctor, but she is less certain about her love of this particular boy. Her two highest priorities, motherhood and location, will be the strongest factors in the decision she makes. Wanting to be a doctor and a mother may lead her to pick a less demanding form of medicine over one that requires being on call 24/7.

No matter what she decides, she will make an impact, and she is wise enough to choose the kind she is most comfortable with even at a young age. You are wise, too. What kind of impact is most meaningful to you, and how can you achieve it with your gifts?

When Others Don't Understand

Her half of the nursing home room was extremely small after she had filled it with the things most valuable to her: two dressers, a TV, photo albums, a powered scooter, a walker, one chair, a bedside toilet, and a small table. Finding space for a guitar was impossible, so my voice would have to do. I could hear the hissing of her roommate's oxygen compressor behind the thin curtain; otherwise, the room was quiet.

From her wrinkled mouth came a voice worn by age. She was almost 98, and her vocal chords had stopped working with the clarity of youth. Wisps of air escaped with each vowel sound, giving the impression that she had a slow leak when she spoke. It seemed the sound of air moving was the melodic theme for any harmonies we would make in this session.

I sang songs of youth, faraway places, and hope to support the stories of her past that she was struggling to tell. As I asked her thoughts on one particular song, she lowered her brow and weakly informed me it was a song for the young. The song was actually very old, so I was puzzled by her response and asked her to explain.

We talked about the theme of hope in the lyrics, and the fatigue showed on her face as she rasped that she was too old for hope these days. My heart deflated, joining the room's symphony of escaping air. Was the hiss in her voice the sound of hers deflating as well?

Like a good therapist, I worked gently with her aching heart, removing layers of explanation and excuse until the truth was beating before us, strong and real. She was tired of living and ready to die. Life had not been bad, but it hadn't been all she had hoped for, either. She had not been alone, but she had not been deeply and passionately loved. She had done much, but now she was finished.

By the end of our time together, her voice was almost gone, and I knew we were done for the day. We had not solved the problems of the world; we had not erased the disappointments that come with 98 years of life. However, this day connecting had a sound: an oxygen machine giving life and a tired, 98-year-old voice saying, "Thank you for taking time to try to understand."

Not everyone could have spent an hour with a depressed, 98-year-old in a nursing home. To me, however, the hour was full of purpose, and her gratitude assured me the time had not been wasted. Even after 12 years as a music therapist, many people still do not understand how or why I do what I do. They see me differently than I see myself, and they have their own dreams for my life.

At an early age, I learned that having public gifts is a blessing as well as a curse. When others think they know what you're good at, they also think they know how you should use those gifts. Public expression of your strengths does not mean the decision about how you use them is open to public debate. Even if your gifts are less public, people who love you will have many grand ideas about what your life should become. I guarantee you there will be people who don't understand the type of impact most meaningful to you.

I still get questions like, "Why aren't you performing full time?" or "When are you making another album?" or "How can you spend time in those terribly depressing places?" or my personal favorite, "Why don't you do something on TV?" People don't mean any harm; many of them love me very much. They are simply imagining the type of impact they would choose to make if they had a monopoly on my gifts. However, they do not have my gifts, and it is up to me to listen for the sounds of success in my life when I start each day.

Any measure of success is accompanied by an equal measure of opposition often coming, unintentionally, from those we love. The people around us want the best for us, or at least the best they can imagine. It is our job to know our gifts and the kind of impact that means the most to us so we can help others imagine our lives the same way we do. When they don't understand, tell them of your passion and what you hold most dear. Show them your gifts in action and the way they can benefit those around you. Whatever you do, don't be angry with them for dreaming on your behalf. Dreams don't really come in large or small sizes; instead, they come in a million different shapes.

Success has a sound. In my life, it includes the sounds of aching hearts and the music that brings them comfort. In your life it may include the laughter of children, the crunch of numbers, the shouts of the stock exchange, the buzz of a pager, or a whisper of gratitude. Whatever your life's pursuits, the sound of success will always include the hum of your unique gifts in action, the beat of your heart fully committed to your cause, the rich harmony of your life contributing to others, and the applause of those who love you no matter what you choose. Enjoy the music!

Lea Mack Compton is an award-winning devotional writer, speaker, and board certified music therapist (MT-BC) with a B.A. in music therapy from Florida State University. She delights in communicating principles of effective living with a variety of audiences through the services offered by her company, Dream Big Enterprises, LLC.

Lea's music therapy work includes hospice patients and their families, school-age children, and senior citizens. She served as Ohio's Junior

Miss 1991 and Miss Ohio 1995 and is now married and living in South Carolina.

26

Dancing with an Impact

Casey Noblett

We were running late. I changed quickly into my costume and made final adjustments, not sparing any time to look around. I failed to notice the Nobel Peace Prize on the mantel on the other side of the room. It wasn't until I ran out the door of the Roosevelt Room and glanced to my right that I saw the Oval Office. It uncharacteristically took my preperformance breath away.

Though I was only 14 years old, it was a moment I would never forget. I stood in the White House on my way to the Rose Garden to perform at a State dinner for President William Jefferson Clinton. My running thought: if all those dreaded ballet classes got me here, then I would take a million more. Though I didn't know it then, the performance was the highlight of my dance career. How could I possibly top dancing for the President of the United States in his home?

Well, life proved that there were many highlights yet in store for me. It was in these early years that I measured success in quantity: how much money I made or how many big shows I performed in, like the one above. Throughout my life my definition of success has evolved; and today, I realize my true success is measured in quality.

I am by every definition a dancer. I grew up training in my mother's dance studio in the small town of Roxboro, NC. When I was nine, famed choreographer and dancer Jacques d'Amboise discovered me in a community class at Duke University and invited me to perform in his show there. After that performance, he gave me the invitation of a lifetime. I was asked to come to New York City, live in his house for the summer, and train at the National Dance Institute's summer intensive. For the next seven summers my mom, eventually my brother, and I packed up and studied in NYC for six weeks. I took ballet with Lori Klinger and tap with Barbara Duffy and jazz with Patti Wilcox and Suzi Taylor. With NDI I performed at The Lincoln Center, Madison Square Garden, The Kennedy Center, The White House, The Smithsonian Institute, and The World Financial Center. I met Gregory Hines and Terrance Mann and was thrown headfirst into the amazing dance community that NYC had to offer. I took as many classes as my body could physically handle and went to Broadway shows on the weekends. In these action-packed summers, I realized dance was my life.

I would return home to my small town of 8,000 people rejuvenated and ready to work. As I aged out of Jacques's program at 16, I knew I needed to continue the intensity of my training, so I attended the North Carolina School of the Arts for my senior year of high school and then attended the New World School of the Arts in Miami for college. Being in a conservatory setting at both institutions fine tuned my technique.

These experiences were so intense, in fact, that I discovered in my freshman year that the back pain that had plagued me for months was in fact three stress fractures in my lower three vertebrae. I thought the pain was a pulled muscle! I decided it was nothing that a little bit of Tylenol and some strong will wouldn't heal. I was not about to take six months off. All I wanted to do was dance.

Once I graduated I began auditioning and dancing in Miami for the Latin television networks Univision and Telemundo. I loved Latin music and dance and had to train additionally, since these were not areas I was proficient in. It was amazing to dance for Gloria

Estefan and Chayanne and for the Latin awards shows. It definitely helped that I spoke Spanish, thanks to a two-week exchange program to Spain in high school. I then performed in a show for Disney in Miami and decided that Orlando would be my next stop.

Disneyworld has amazing opportunities for dancers, and I longed for a steady paycheck. I auditioned and instead of landing a spot on the main castle stage, I got asked to go to Japan and dance at Tokyo Disneyland for seven months. This was not my plan, but I was up for the challenge. I had danced in Taiwan with my college dance company and loved Asia, so I knew it would be an adventure.

Adventure it was. I loved every minute of it, although dancing in the same show five times a day, five days a week (a grand total of 600 shows for the contract) was taxing on my body and my mind. I headed back to Florida in search of something new.

Upon my return, I opted for a new spin on dance. I auditioned for and made it onto the NBA's Atlanta Hawks Dance Team. Not only was I able to perform, but I also began teaching for local studios, as well as choreographing for the team. I also worked with new and upcoming artists, which Atlanta is known for producing. I was meeting new people, staying busy, and always looking for more opportunities.

Because I started a dance career at such a young age, I always had dreams of fame and fortune. I thought that with those dreams achieved, I would truly be happy and feel successful. I loved being in the spotlight or walking into a television studio and having the team of make-up artists get me ready for my dance number. It was so exciting to see different parts of the world and meet famous people along the way. Though my résumé grew longer with each new job, my sheer determination drove me to try to get ten more gigs.

Although these years were filled with ambition and excitement, I always felt unfulfilled. I constantly compared myself to other dancers. Were they better than me? What cool jobs were they doing that I wasn't? Why didn't I get to go on tour with a popular artist? These questions always left me frustrated. I never felt truly content with my own career, even though I was doing great. Someone looking in on my life would have thought that I was very successful, but I didn't feel that way. It was so hard to avoid the jealousy, knowing that someone out there was doing bigger and better things than I was.

I needed something that would incorporate dance as well as give me a way to excel and achieve my own personal goals, without comparing them to others. I decided to try a different outlet to find true happiness and success. I always needed more money, as we dancers do, and looked for a way to expand on the classes I had been teaching at studios all over the Southeast. I found that when I went to teach, studio owners often asked if I knew a good tap teacher or a good modern teacher. I knew ten good modern teachers! So I began to compile photos and résumés of all my dancer friends whom I had worked with along the way, including my mom and brother, Cassidy, who was now dancing professionally in NYC and LA. I then started to develop weekend workshops that included teachers other than myself. I would take friends with me to teach, and I created weekend intensives rather than just master classes.

In 2001, N-House Productions was born, and I was creating conventions, taught by me and my colleagues, all over the country for dancers of all ages and abilities. It was not easy to build a company from the ground up with few clients and little money for advertising. I worked hard because I had time and not a lot of money. I spent hours and hours on the Internet to find studios. By sending email advertisements rather than magazine ads, I was able to reach potential customers for very little overhead. Eventually, my business grew, and we traveled to more cities and taught more young dancers. I soon had 20 employees all over the country teaching and choreographing with and for me at these conventions.

At first, I was a driven businesswoman: I wanted N-House to take off. I had started the company to further my exposure in the dance community, as well as to provide a steady income for myself. Along the way, something happened that I never expected. As I met these dancers, mostly from small studios in small towns, I began to realize what an impact we made by being there. I would bring in teachers and the cream-of-the-crop professionals—Broadway performers or music video dancers—to work with these dancers, who saw the dance profession as out of their reach as a career. I saw energy and excitement and their love of dance pour through their movements. I began to love the interaction with the dancers much more than the paycheck I received at the conclusion of the workshop.

After about two years of being in business, an email from one of the students I had taught stopped me in my tracks. It read: "I wanted to tell you how much of an impact you have made, not just in my dancing experience, but in my life. I thank you for giving me a chance to be noticed. I hope you understand how much you have changed me and my love for dance. I truly know now what I want to do in the future."

As I sat there and read those words, I began to see what really mattered: this one student. In just 48 hours with us, we made a difference in her life. Somewhere within all the dance instruction, we were able to instill confidence in this talented, but somehow overlooked, young dancer. I had given her the push she needed to realize her dreams.

I now receive three or four of these emails each year, and they are truly my prized possessions. They remind me of why I do what I do. I realize that few people will remember what performances I was in, but how many dancers will remember the classes I taught?

I had started a company to help boost my ego and my income but came away with something much richer. Although I still perform occasionally, I now understand that my personal success is defined by lives that I influence, one dancer at a time.

In my office, I keep a short parable to remind me about what it really means to be successful. Any day that I am frustrated with my job or need to be reminded of why I teach, this story helps me to recognize what really matters in my life:

Every morning an old man walked down the beach picking up starfish that had washed up in the night. Slowly, carefully, one by one, he threw them back into the ocean beyond the breakers. One day a young man walked up to him and asked, "Old man, why do you throw these starfish back, day after day? There are thousands of them. You'll never make a difference." The old man picked up a starfish, threw it back into the ocean, and said, "It makes a difference to this one."

Casey began dancing under the direction of her mother, Toni Noblett, in Roxboro, NC. She later studied with Jacques d'Amboise in New York City and continued her classical training at the North Carolina School of the Arts and New World School of the Arts in Miami, FL.

Casey's stage credits include performances at The White House and Kennedy Center for President Bill Clinton; The Lincoln Center; Madison Square Garden; The World Financial Center; and The Smithsonian Institute. She has performed internationally at Tokyo Disneyland, in Kaohsiung, Taiwan, and at the NBA's Jam Session in Caracas, Venezuela as captain of the Atlanta Hawks Dance Team.

Casey's television credits include work with artists such as Gloria Estefan, Will Smith, and Chayanne, as well as performances on Extreme Home Makeover, MTV, CBS, and the Latin networks Univision and Telemundo. Casey has also been involved in the launch of new artists Third Phaze, Sixx Carter, and Ayanna.

Casey was named North Carolina's Junior Miss and second runner-up at AJM in 1997. She has since been a choreographer, production director, and judge with North Carolina and Georgia's Junior Miss programs.

Casey is the owner and director of N-House Productions and teaches and choreographs year-round at studios and universities across the U.S. and Canada.

4

Conclusion

27

The Sum of Our Success

Amy E. Goodman

Fifty contestants swarmed the stage dressed in caps and gowns to represent our newly graduated selves. A moving collage of hugs and smiles and early farewells, we whispered excitedly, taking our marks for the opening number. Energy swayed around us like a heady, sweaty-palmed partner. We wondered, who would make finalist? Who would be 1991 America's Junior Miss?

I sat down to take it all in. I felt energized for others but not ecstatic for myself. I hailed from California—a big state known for big wins—but I hadn't won a single preliminary award. Even I had my favorite, and it wasn't me.

As a dutiful overachiever of 18 years of age, I'd doled significant effort and emotion into preparing for the program. So had my other 49 brilliant, college-bound sisters, one representing each state. None of us was accustomed to coming in second place, let alone no place at all; and in a moment's time a whole bunch of us would feel an unabashed smack of disappointment. I asked myself: Could I possibly be cool with walking away with *nothing*? Was this a defining moment for someone, but *not me*?

Without hesitation, yes, my answer was yes. The relief was immediate. My nerves calmed, my flush cooled, and I felt at peace. No one thing would define me, I decided. Would I win this? No. Could I possibly achieve other things? You bet.

If no one thing delivers guaranteed happiness—no amount of money, no prestigious diploma, no lofty job, no scholarship honor— then what defines a successful person? For me, a life richly lived through every age and course of action is wherein success lies. In my case this has been achieved by building a sound identity (by embracing what makes me different and developing a strong work ethic) as a girl; by learning to love myself and define my passions as a young woman; and by creating a professional life for which I was prepared and in which I could both uplift and be uplifted.

Embrace Your Differences

When you're a kid, everyone assumes that life is easy. You brown bag it to school or plunk down change for a hot lunch, you ride the bus (hopefully a hump seat above the wheel), and you learn your ABC's and 123's. On a hot day, you beg for ice cream. On a cold day, you beg for ice cream. Pretty easy breezy, right?

Funny, but I remember the early years as a bit more complicated than that. It was a time to lay a foundation and begin to crack the shell of who I was. This of course went beyond the question of whether I preferred Gobstoppers or Lemon Heads. Serious questions about identity and differences popped up early that needed answers, followed by some early indicators that hard work was about to become my new, best adolescent friend.

When I was a young lass, I knew that I thought differently from my peers. An only child and wise beyond my baby-doll bangs, I commented to my father after the first day of kindergarten, "The kids act like such children! Why can't they just grow up?"

Not only did I have a challenge in relating to kiddos my age, but I also discovered that there were other notable differences. What other children had rice balls stuffed with fish eggs and pickled plums in their lunch box? Who else rushed home on a blistering California day, only to throw on a kimono and practice Japanese tea ceremony for three hours atop hard straw mats? Did other kids get pulled out of school for months at a time to study the art of classical dancing ... *in Japan?*

As a Japanese-American girl with a Tokyo-born mother and a meat-and-potatoes-bred Oregonian father, I stood out a tad in a relatively milk-colored school. It wasn't so much my looks, but rather, my little Asian attitude that set me apart on the playground: a deep pride my parents instilled to never cower from my ethnicity.

This meant practicing Japanese dance from the age of two and a half and receiving my professional dancing name by the age of 16; starting Japanese tea ceremony by age six; attending Japanese school on Saturdays at the Buddhist temple; and joyfully eating smelly, salty fish with my mother, while my father stood outside on the deck until we finished.

It was a dual life. Yet, I seamlessly switched between speaking Japanese and English and regularly entertained the community or classmates with dance performances complete with kimonos, wigs, and white makeup.

In high school, I had a fellow Asian friend who asked if I ever struggled with "the balancing act" between both cultures. In my case, it wasn't an act. It was simply never a question. Under the firm rule of my mother, who doubled as my dance and tea instructor, and with traditional Japanese grandparents who lived nearby, visited often, and filled our home with the delicious flavors of Nippon, I had a strong lineage of proud immigrants who celebrated their culture and preserved it in everyday life through food, ritual, and custom.

As a child, you do what your parents say because you have no choice. From a young age, however, I was cognizant of my choice to embrace what made me unique and thus danced and stamped my little Japanese feet to my heart's content.

Identify what makes you different, whether it is your ethnicity or a different way of dressing. Explore. Then come dance with me.

Buzz Like the Busiest of Bees

First period my senior year of high school: AP Biology. First row. Slumped in my chair, surrounded by two backpacks and homework, I wearily thought about the long day ahead. I was always tired both physically and mentally, and sometimes during videos of wasps or fruit flies or separating chromosomes, I'd fall asleep.

In high school, like in natural selection, there were two types of successful students: those who didn't need to study to ace tests and those who did a fair amount of work for above average results. Forever the anomaly, I constituted my own category: the kid who burned the midnight oil. I set school records studying through the night in order to get the grades I wanted. For unlike the naturally smart kids or ones who moderately exercised their brains for decent grades, I needed to work hard, really hard, to compensate for my lack of natural abilities.

The discipline from dance and tea came in handy. A stern pair of eyes looking over my shoulder—my Japanese grandfather, Grandpa Ginji—didn't hurt, either. Once in junior high school I handed him my straight-A report card. He looked it over and handed it back. "Next time, you'll do better," he replied.

Was he joking? Not really. He knew, as we all do, that discipline and determination pay off and that one shouldn't be merely satisfied with making the grade. I really needed to absorb what I learned beyond a letter on a report card. This was what prepared me for a life's worth of learning to come.

Like a focused bee, I buzzed my way through high school, toiling over stacks of homework and difficult assignments, finding that relentless hard work was my best flight plan to developing a thriving educational garden. All of us have our ways of getting the job done, and developing your own routine early on when your brain is fresh and new will lay a smooth foundation for learning for the years ahead.

Declare Yourself: Life beyond High School

There will come a time when your parents or caregivers are no longer your number-one cheerleaders, and what's left is you and your mirrored reflection. After graduations from middle school, high school, and college, there won't be risers filled with your fans screaming your name to victory. Of course, your family will always be your private entourage to support you, but there will come a time when you'll be alone. This moment, when fully realized, perhaps while sitting on the floor of your first unfurnished apartment, is a scary one. You are now the queen bee, sitting atop a honeycomb of degrees—and, Honey, guess what? It's time to make some.

Some of you will sigh with relief ("Yes! I'll finally be on my own!"), but the crux of the matter is that growing up and the pains that come with it seriously unsettle the system.

This is the one thing that no one told me during my entire college career at University of California at Los Angeles: how difficult my twenties would be. Armed with an invincible attitude (hey, I was the Administrative Vice President for over 25,000 undergraduate students!), a *summa cum laude* degree in Communications, and a spackling of other college honors and job experiences, I felt that nothing could get in my way of living a dream, any dream. It's the great American way! I was going to make it happen!

Then I sat up in the corner of that empty apartment. What was I going to make happen, exactly? Put a little self-love in that heart.

After a deep conversation with my soul and a mountain of frozen yogurt later, I tried to determine any regrets: was there anything missing from life *now* (other than more soft-serve yogurt) that I'd mourn the lack of later? College offers an unparalleled opportunity to unearth your queries about the world, and I was too young to have inquisitive regrets. I decided that I might as well figure out what they were and stamp them out fast, like a controlled wildfire.

A bowl of noodles later and I had it. I'd missed the opportunity to study abroad.

Just so I didn't give my parents a complete heart attack, the summer between my sophomore and junior years I *did* study at the Sorbonne in Paris, France—trying to cram a year's experience into a 10-week program. But I'd always wanted the luxury of a bigger block of time to embrace a country, and now was my chance.

My first year in Japan I was a scholarship student of Japanese tea ceremony with the Urasenke School of Tea in Japan. Studying this traditional art form from its source in Kyoto was a year of enlightenment, extreme discipline, and enrichment: but still, I craved more. I followed this with a second year abroad in Fukuyama, Japan as an English teacher with the Japanese government's JET Programme.

Two years away from family and friends and regular shoulders to lean on. Two years uprooted from the comfortable collegiate campus of which I knew every square inch. These were years of prodding my comfort zone—of learning to live on my own, of trying to convince stalwart sushi chefs to make vegetarian sushi, of developing a *path of most resistance*, to see what part of me pushed back.

Slowly, a shift occurred. I felt less reliant on comforting words from overseas telephone calls. When I didn't understand my convoluted electric bill, I figured it out. Even during dark days (like when I learned I had frostbitten toes from a cold apartment), a new cheering section began to appear.

I stepped before the mirror and laughed. I was a roaring cheerleader of one.

This paradigm upheaval towards complete independence combined with the matured appreciation to enjoy it will happen to each in her own stead. You might be sixteen and working through high school when it hits you. You might be in college when you feel your own support system start to kick in. Whenever it happens, you'll feel the inner strength of pure self-love and how buoyant it makes you feel. You'll realize how less reliant you are on adulation from others to get you through the less-than-stellar moments.

You'll hear her when you've found her, because she'll be screaming loudly from your heart that though the world is rough, you're OK.

Fly with Your Passion

It was during this technologically primitive time in Japan— pre-Internet calling, pre-instant messaging, pre-You Tubing—when I started writing. I mean, really spilling the ink. I'd pound out emails from the moment I got home until well past bedtime. I'd drag my then-heavy laptop in a backpack up 12% grade hills on my bicycle to whichever school I was working at so that I could write during breaks. I started short stories, essays, and even chapters of a novel. I typed so hard for so long that holding a pen felt primitive.

As I began to think of life beyond Japan, one thing became achingly clear. All those stories I wrote in elementary school? About a frog who went to college? A typed, 12-page novel I wrote in the fourth grade titled "Ginnyham Junction?" My preference for written over Scantron tests in college? My prolific journaling in Fukuyama? All of this was pointing to a career in writing.

During this preelectronic period, I had a typewriter sent over from the U.S. and applied to journalism schools right away. This untrained author, who'd never slaved on a high school yearbook committee or toiled on the staff of her college paper, was accepted to Columbia University's School of Journalism.

Sure. Some people are born knowing they want to clone kidneys, research alternative fuel sources, raise families, or do a combination thereof, but my process of finding what made me tick was a long, unexpected journey. Never be discouraged if your light bulb hasn't flickered until well after college (or if it flicks several times and you have multiple careers). Don't let concerned parents ("Haven't you decided YET?") pressure you into making a selection that would better please them than you. It's best to wait until you have your revelation rather than wander onto a divergent path that leaves you directionless.

The electrifying moment I thought, *Wouldn't it be great if I could make a career out of writing?* was the moment my heart started flying.

Happily, it's still soaring.

Flex Your Wings: Make the Working World Work for You

Just before my year-intensive graduate program was over, I began the job hunt for a career in magazines. As an Asian American Journalists Association member, I received a posting for an editorial assistant at *In Style* magazine. After a laborious interview process over a couple of months, I received a call on my cell phone, while I was touring the Statue of Liberty: I got the job.

Thus began a felicitous eight-year tenure with the magazine and a successful freelance career as a writer and broadcaster thereafter. But I do recall the less-than-glamorous moment when, in my flannel pjs and perched atop a phonebook on a tipsy vinyl chair, I'd spotted that original *In Style* posting. What a great chance, I told myself: an entry-level position in which I could grow. But how do I do this with no formal journalism experience? How do I prove that I am ready for this opportunity? What do I do now?

Know Your Audience

After printing my résumé and copying my writing samples, I headed to the New York City public library. At that time, *In Style* approached its fifth year of publication, and I intended to arm myself with as much knowledge about the magazine as possible.

Over that weekend, I set up shop in the archives department and proceeded to read nearly every issue of *In Style* ever printed. Then I crafted my cover letter to reflect my research, dropped off my packet in person at Time Inc. (the magazine's publisher), and received a response a day later to come in for an interview.

Now arguably, reading every past issue was a bit much, but for me it was the preparation I felt was necessary to become the best candidate. Know whom you are dealing with: know the product, know the audience/consumer, and get a sense for the creators. It was through the Managing Editor's letter that I saw pictures of the staff, and through the masthead that I understood its evolution. Before ever interviewing, I tried to imagine the people who worked there and then me working alongside them.

Later, as an Associate Editor with *In Style*, I'd hire interns for my department, upon whom a great deal of responsibility was demanded. It shocked me, the number of interviews I'd need to conduct before finding a viable candidate. I lamented the college graduates with stellar grade point averages who lacked preparation, with their misguided notion that their "love for the magazine" would get them hired. But what did they love?

In the same way that you'd prepare for a test, take time to prep for an interview. Do the research to know as much about the company culture as you can. Arm yourself with examples as to why you'd like to be hired aside from a hollow promise of simply "loving the company." If you can answer why you are the best suited for the position, why you envision yourself as compatible with your future coworkers, and why you foresee the company benefiting from your hire, then you are worthy to sit down and commence the interview.

Carry Others with You

After all of the hard work to obtain and maintain your job, one might wonder why you'd lend a hand to the next person who wants your position. Why make it easier for others when your personal journey was so difficult?

When I worked at *In Style,* the "I'm your friend X's cousin and I want a job" emails would number 3–4 a week. To this day, I still receive inquiries from friends, strangers, and friends of strangers about working at the magazine. It's a popular place, and everyone fresh out of college—and not so fresh out of college—wants to work there.

It would be far easier for me to simply forward these inquiries to human resources. But as much as possible, I respond with as much specificity as I have time for, in an attempt to give them enough information to be a strong candidate for consideration.

I've never understood the concept of not helping people progress professionally (or personally, for that matter), especially when you are in a position to do so. Yes, publishing is competitive. Yes, the industry can get ugly. Does that mean I need to participate? Perpetuate? Absolutely not. And in your relative industry, you need not, either.

You *can* carry people with you in your professional journey. As you rise in your industry, as you excel by your smarts, you can enjoy the ride with others rather than push your competitors down. There is room for everyone to stand at the top. I've helped strangers, friends, family, and even my enemies along my way.

Enemies? I hear you asking. *What good does that do?*

In the grand scheme of things, life is not a solo effort. We are interconnected—and the more we help each other the faster we grow as a whole. Helping those who dislike you can be healing, and throughout my experiences I've never regretted taking the higher road, ever.

Be Prepared for the Unexpected

A couple of years into my stint at *In Style*, the Managing Editor tapped me to do television. I was an on-air editor promoting the magazine in whatever capacity was needed: talking about celebrity lifestyle, fashion, beauty products, entertaining, gifts for Mother's Day, etc. First I started on local networks and the CNN airport circuit. Then soon after I tackled live national segments on the *Today Show, Good Morning America, The View,* and others, eventually becoming the face of *In Style*.

Aside from the initial dream of writing, I found that television satisfied yet a different aspect of my journalistic hunger. Though unintended, I'd grown another branch of my career when I wasn't looking, and it had flourished.

Now, as a freelancer living in Washington, DC, my broadcast endeavors are a primary focus. I host a couple of local shows, fly everywhere else for segments, and maintain my appearances regularly on national outlets. With two young children, this newfound career fits well into our nanny-free lifestyle, where I try my best to be a very present force in their lives. Granted, I have to travel for what I do, but I always return for long stints at home to cook dinner, plant the garden, and harvest the daily delights in watching my children grow.

I look back on the trajectory of my life to date, and I simply never would've imagined it: that I would live abroad in Japan for two years, live in New York City for six, and then relinquish the fast-paced Manhattan lifestyle to shelter in the suburbs of Washington, DC (with a husband, house, fence, dog, and cat). Somehow, no amount of forethought could have prepared me this—and for signing my first book contract with Atria, an imprint of Simon & Schuster as I write.

I've embraced the unexpected and relinquished my heart to not forcing or hurrying the future. The flexibility of not knowing what lies ahead gives me greater freedom to focus on this moment. I hear the seconds ticking, do you?

The Final Word

As every unique snowflake falls perfectly in space and time as it's meant to, so too has my life been my journey and mine alone. Along that path some universal truths emerged that, though obvious to some, served as important discoveries to me and thus hopefully to you. To summarize, remember to embrace your differences and maintain a focused work ethic; inject your heart with self-love and pursue your passion; and prepare for professional life, prepare for the unexpected, and help people in your endeavors, as there is room for everyone at the top.

A few cell phones, Discmans, and wrinkles ago, the name of the 1991 AJM winner was announced amidst pounding hearts, hopeful dreams, and stage lights hotter than the Malibu sun. Nervous limbs shook and the audience gasped as seven finalists were whittled down to three (drum roll please), one of whom was the dark horse: Me.

It doesn't matter whose name was ultimately called. It doesn't matter that amidst the din and cacophony I didn't hear the final proclamation. What did matter was the peace agreement I'd made with myself at the start of the show that no one title would determine my future course.

Therein lies the secret: we are the sum of our success.

Amy E. Goodman has a rich editorial history with women's magazines, working as a freelancer for In Style, Latina, Real Simple, Women's Health, All You, DC's The Magazine Group, *and* MSNBC. com. *A diverse general reporter, she has an extensive breadth of coverage including fashion and red carpet, beauty and health, fitness and food, home and entertaining, and celebrity news for such broadcast outlets as* ET, Access Hollywood, NBC'S Today, E!, Fox & Friends, *and* VH1, *among others. Currently, she is Fashion Trend Director for TIMEX and host of Washington Flyer TV.*

Goodman has been a spokesperson for such corporate entities as Spanx, Baskin Robbins, and Level Vodka. With *TBS's* Movie and a Makeover, *she has done spotlights for Wal-Mart, Hasbro, and Payless Shoes. In 2004, she was selected from 100 candidates by At the Beach Productions and First Light Pictures to be the host of an eponymous-titled pilot,* On the Road . . . with Amy G.

During her pregnancy, she was signed with NYC's Expecting Models Agency. Health *magazine featured Goodman in its May 2007 issue. She served as a correspondent for* In Style Magazine, *where she was part of the editorial staff beginning in June 1999. Over her eight-year tenure with the magazine, Goodman was responsible for conceptualizing, producing, reporting, and writing celebrity lifestyle stories. In addition, she served as a regular, on-air Contributing Editor for* The Today Show, Good Morning Ameria, The Early Show, The View, CNN, Extra, ABC's World News Now, *and affiliates of ABC, NBC, CBS and FOX.*

Previous to her work at In Style, *Goodman was a member of the editorial team at* Parents Magazine. *She also spent two years in Japan, where she was an English teacher and studied the art of Japanese tea ceremony.*

In 1991, Goodman was selected from over 2,000 young women nationwide to hold the title of America's Junior Miss (AJM). In 2007, she cohosted the 50th Anniversary program of AJM in Mobile, AL.

Goodman graduated Phi Beta Kappa and summa cum laude *with a B.A. in Communications and Foreign Languages from the University of California at Los Angeles. She holds a master's degree in Journalism from Columbia University's Graduate School of Journalism. A native of Santa Rosa, CA, she currently resides in Washington, DC with her husband and two children.*

Breinigsville, PA USA
28 February 2011
256552BV00001B/1/P